EMMA LAZARUS

EMMA LAZARUS

DIANE LEFER

CHELSEA HOUSE PUBLISHERS

NEW YORK • NEW HAVEN • PHILADELPHIA

Lazarus

EDITOR-IN-CHIEF: Nancy Toff
EXECUTIVE EDITOR: Remmel T. Nunn
MANAGING EDITOR: Karyn Gullen Browne
COPY CHIEF: Juliann Barbato
PICTURE EDITOR: Adrian G. Allen
ART DIRECTOR: Giannella Garrett
MANUFACTURING MANAGER: Gerald Levine

Staff for EMMA LAZARUS

SENIOR EDITOR: Constance Jones
ASSISTANT EDITOR: Maria Behan
COPYEDITOR: Ellen Scordato
EDITORIAL ASSISTANT: Theodore Keyes
PICTURE RESEARCHER: Monica Gannon
DESIGNER: Design Oasis
PRODUCTION COORDINATOR: Joseph Romano
COVER ILLUSTRATION: Eva Auchincloss

CREATIVE DIRECTOR: Harold Steinberg

First Printing

1 3 5 7 9 8 6 4 2

Library of Congress Cataloging in Publication Data

Lefer, Diane.
Emma Lazarus.

(American women of achievement)
Bibliography: p.
Includes index.
Summary: A biography of the nineteenth-century American poet
best known for the verses inscribed on the pedestal of the Statue
of Liberty.
1. Lazarus, Emma, 1849–1887—Biography—Juvenile literature. 2.
Poets, American—19th century—Biography—Juvenile
literature. [1. Lazarus, Emma, 1849–1887. 2. Poets, American] I.
Title. II. Series.
PS2234.L44 1988   811'.4 [B] [92]   87-21849
ISBN 1-55546-664-8

CONTENTS

AMERICAN WOMEN of ACHIEVEMENT

Abigail Adams
women's rights activist

Jane Addams
social worker

Louisa May Alcott
author

Marian Anderson
singer

Susan B. Anthony
woman suffragist

Ethel Barrymore
actress

Clara Barton
*founder of the American
Red Cross*

Elizabeth Blackwell
physician

Nellie Bly
journalist

Margaret Bourke-White
photographer

Pearl Buck
author

Rachel Carson
biologist and author

Mary Cassatt
painter

Agnes De Mille
choreographer

Emily Dickinson
poet

Isadora Duncan
dancer

Amelia Earhart
aviator

Mary Baker Eddy
*founder of the Christian
Science church*

Betty Friedan
feminist

Althea Gibson
tennis champion

Emma Goldman
revolutionary

Helen Hayes
actress

Lillian Hellman
playwright

Katharine Hepburn
actress

Karen Horney
psychoanalyst

Anne Hutchinson
religious leader

Mahalia Jackson
gospel singer

Helen Keller
humanitarian

Jeane Kirkpatrick
diplomat

Emma Lazarus
poet

Clare Boothe Luce
author and diplomat

Barbara McClintock
biologist

Margaret Mead
anthropologist

Edna St. Vincent Millay
poet

Julia Morgan
architect

Grandma Moses
painter

Louise Nevelson
sculptor

Sandra Day O'Connor
Supreme Court Justice

Georgia O'Keeffe
painter

Eleanor Roosevelt
diplomat and humanitarian

Wilma Rudolph
champion athlete

Florence Sabin
physician

Beverly Sills
singer

Gertrude Stein
author

Gloria Steinem
feminist

Harriet Beecher Stowe
author and abolitionist

Mae West
entertainer

Edith Wharton
author

Phillis Wheatley
poet

Babe Zaharias
champion athlete

CHELSEA HOUSE PUBLISHERS

"Remember the Ladies"

MATINA S. HORNER

Remember the Ladies." That is what Abigail Adams wrote to her husband John, then a delegate to the Continental Congress, as the Founding Fathers met in Philadelphia to form a new nation in March of 1776. "Be more generous and favorable to them than your ancestors. Do not put such unlimited power in the hands of the Husbands. If particular care and attention is not paid to the Ladies," Abigail Adams warned, "we are determined to foment a Rebellion, and will not hold ourselves bound by any Laws in which we have no voice, or Representation."

The words of Abigail Adams, one of the earliest American advocates of women's rights, were prophetic. Because when we have not "remembered the ladies," they have, by their words and deeds, reminded us so forcefully of the omission that we cannot fail to remember them. For the history of American women is as interesting and varied as the history of our nation as a whole. American women have played an integral part in founding, settling, and building our country. Some we remember as remarkable women who—against great odds—achieved distinction in the public arena: Anne Hutchinson, who in the 17th century became a charismatic religious leader; Phillis Wheatley, an 18th-century black slave who became a poet; Susan B. Anthony, whose name is synonymous with the 19th-century women's rights movement, and who led the struggle to enfranchise women; and, in our own century, Amelia Earhart, the first woman to cross the Atlantic Ocean by air.

These extraordinary women certainly merit our admiration, but other women, "common women," many of them all but forgotten, should also be recognized for their contributions to American thought and culture. Women have been community builders; they have founded schools and formed voluntary associations to help those in need; they have assumed the major responsibility for rearing children, passing on from one generation to the next the values that keep a culture alive. These and innumerable other contributions, once ignored, are now being recognized by scholars, students, and the public. It is exciting and gratifying to realize that a part of our history that was hardly acknowledged a few generations ago is now being studied and brought to light.

In recent decades, the field of women's history has grown from obscurity to a politically controversial splinter movement to academic respectability, in many cases mainstreamed into such traditional disciplines as history, economics, and psychology. Scholars of women, both female and male, have organized research centers at such prestigious institutions as Wellesley College, Stanford University, and the University of California. Other notable centers for women's studies are the Center for the American Woman and Politics at the Eagleton Institute of Politics at Rutgers University, the Henry A. Murray Research Center for the Study of Lives, at Radcliffe College, and the Women's Research and Education Institute, the research arm of the Congressional Caucus on Women's Issues. Other scholars and public figures have established archives and libraries, such as the Schlesinger Library on the History of Women in America, at Radcliffe College, and the Sophia Smith Collection, at Smith College, to collect and preserve the written and tangible legacies of women.

From the initial donation of the Women's Rights Collection in 1943, the Schlesinger Library grew to encompass vast collections documenting the manifold accomplishments of American women. Simultaneously, the women's movement in general and the academic discipline of women's studies in particular also began with a narrow definition and gradually expanded their mandate. Early causes such as woman suffrage and social reform, abolition and organized labor were joined by newer concerns such as the history of women in business and the professions and in politics and government; the study of the family; and social issues such as health policy and education.

Women, as historian Arthur M. Schlesinger, jr., once pointed out, "have constituted the most spectacular casualty of traditional history. They have made up at least half the human race, but you could never tell that by looking at the books historians write." The new breed of historians is remedying that omission. They have written books about immigrant women and about working-class women who struggled for survival in cities and about black women who met the challenges of life in rural areas. They are telling the stories of women who, despite the barriers of tradition and economics, became lawyers and doctors and public figures.

The women's studies movement has also led scholars to question traditional interpretations of their respective disciplines. For example, the study of war has traditionally been an exercise in military and political analysis, an examination of strategies planned and executed by men. But scholars of women's history have pointed out that wars have also been periods of tremendous change and even opportunity for women, because the very absence of men on the home front enabled them to expand their educational, economic, and professional activities and to assume leadership in their homes.

The early scholars of women's history showed a unique brand of courage in choosing to investigate new subjects and take new approaches to old ones. Often, like their subjects, they endured criticism and even ostracism by their academic colleagues. But their efforts have unquestionably been worthwhile, because with the publication of each new study and book another piece of the historical patchwork is sewn into place, revealing an increasingly comprehensive picture of the role of women in our rich and varied history.

Such books on groups of women are essential, but books that focus on the lives of individuals are equally indispensable. Biographies can be inspirational, offering their readers the example of people with vision who have looked outside themselves for their goals and have often struggled against great obstacles to achieve them. Marian Anderson, for instance, had to overcome racial bigotry in order to perfect her art and perform as a concert singer. Isadora Duncan defied the rules of classical dance to find true artistic freedom. Jane Addams had to break down society's notions of the proper role for women in order to create new social institutions, notably the settlement house. All of these women had to come to terms both with themselves and with the world in which they lived. Only then could they move ahead as pioneers in their chosen callings.

Biography can inspire not only by adulation but also by realism. It helps us to see not only the qualities in others that we hope to emulate, but also, perhaps, the weaknesses that made them "human." By helping us identify with the subject on a more personal level they help us to feel that we, too, can achieve such goals. We read about Eleanor Roosevelt, for instance, who occupied a unique and seemingly enviable position as the wife of the president. Yet we can sympathize with her inner dilemma: an inherently shy woman, she had to force herself to live a most public life in order to use her position to benefit others. We may not be able to imagine ourselves having the immense poetic talent of Emily Dickinson, but from her story we can understand the challenges faced by a creative woman who was expected to fulfill many family responsibilities. And though few of us will ever reach the level of athletic accomplishment displayed by Wilma Rudolph or Babe Zaharias, we can still appreciate their spirit, their overwhelming will to excel.

A biography is a multifaceted lens. It is first of all a magnification, the intimate examination of one particular life. But at the same time, it is a wide-angle lens, informing us about the world in which the subject lived. We come away from reading about one life knowing more about the social, political, and economic fabric of the time. It is for this reason, perhaps, that the great New England essayist Ralph Waldo Emerson wrote, in 1841, "There is properly no history: only biography." And it is also why biography, and particularly women's biography, will continue to fascinate writers and readers alike.

EMMA
LAZARUS

Emma Lazarus was already a well-respected poet when she wrote her tribute to Frédéric-Auguste Bartholdi's statue Liberty Enlightening the World in 1883. Today, that poem, "The New Colossus," is her most celebrated work.

ONE

"Mother of Exiles"

William Maxwell Evarts, former U.S. secretary of state and future senator from New York, seldom had difficulty persuading people to help him. But in 1883, when he asked Emma Lazarus for a favor, she refused him. In Paris, the sculptor Frédéric-Auguste Bartholdi was rapidly completing a work commissioned by the people of France as a gift to the United States, a statue called *Liberty Enlightening the World*. Concerned because America had not yet raised enough money to build the pedestal that the monument would stand on, Evarts asked several eminent writers to compose original poems and stories, which would be sold at an auction in New York City as part of a fundraising drive. Along with Mark Twain and Walt Whitman, Laz-

arus was one of the authors Evarts approached for the project.

The 34-year-old poet and essayist was a logical choice to write a poem for the auction. Not only was she famous throughout America, but she was especially popular in her native New York City, where the monument would eventually be erected. Her first book of verse had appeared when she was still in her teens, and several well-received volumes of poetry and prose had followed. In addition, Lazarus was wealthy and known for her generous contributions to charity.

Nonetheless, Lazarus was unwilling to comply with Evarts's request. She believed that poetry was created out of inspiration and was doubtful of her ability to write anything worthwhile on

American politician William Maxwell Evarts headed a drive to raise money for the pedestal of Bartholdi's statue, which we know today as the Statue of Liberty. When he asked Lazarus to contribute a poem to the project, she initially refused because she disliked writing on demand.

member of the fundraising committee did not. Constance Cary Harrison appealed to the reluctant poet's emotions, encouraging her to think of what the statue might mean to Russia's beleaguered refugees as they saw it for the first time. "The shaft sped home," Mrs. Harrison later reported. "Her dark eyes deepened—her cheek flushed," and Emma Lazarus promised to write a poem about the statue. The fundraising auction was set for early December. In November, with time running out, Emma Lazarus sat down at her desk to keep her word.

Her earliest verses had been based on themes from Greek mythology and the legends of medieval Europe. This strong classical background surfaced when she decided to contrast Bartholdi's sculpture with one of the seven wonders of the ancient world— a huge statue of the Greek god Helios, called Colossus, that was said to have straddled the harbor at Rhodes. But by 1883 Lazarus no longer believed that a reference to past grandeur was enough to make a work great. She knew that her poem would have to look far beyond ancient Greece to express her thoughts about liberty.

demand. She was also very busy working for a cause of her own: helping the thousands of Jews who had fled oppression in Russia and were arriving in New York homeless, penniless, and without prospects.

Evarts finally gave up on enlisting Lazarus in his cause, but another

Once it would have been easy for her to write a piece in which liberty was portrayed as an exalted ideal that transcended daily life in the same way that the statue *Liberty Enlightening the World*, 151 feet high, would tower over

A sketch of the Statue of Liberty adorns the front cover of the catalogue for the Pedestal Fund Art Loan Exhibition. Eminent writers such as Walt Whitman and Mark Twain joined Lazarus in composing original works for the occasion.

This tapestry portrays the Colossus of Rhodes, an enormous statue that was one of the seven wonders of the ancient world. In "The New Colossus," Lazarus contrasted Bartholdi's statue, which she saw as a symbol of welcome, with this "brazen giant."

the ships and people of New York. But clever images and highflown abstractions no longer seemed powerful enough for her purposes.

Lazarus could trace her family tree all the way back to colonial days, but as she sat down to write, even thoughts about the glorious dawn of American independence did not satisfy her. A poem on liberty might refer to the Declaration of Independence and the U.S. Constitution, but precious as those documents were, they did not reveal the human story of America that Emma Lazarus wanted to tell.

As she tried to imagine the completed statue, standing majestically on its pedestal on Bedloe's (now Liberty) Island, in her mind's eye she saw another island altogether: Ward's Island, where it would be hard to find any trace of beauty or majesty at all.

A small square of land lying close by the Manhattan shoreline in the East River, Ward's Island was the site of the city asylum for the insane and the city's "potter's field"—the cemetery for unclaimed corpses and for paupers whose families could not afford to pay for burials. More recently the island had housed thousands of sick and destitute immigrants who had not passed inspection at Castle Garden, the United States immigration station (Ellis Island did not open until 1982). Men, women, and children lived there in temporary barracks as they waited for the U.S. government to determine their fates. Their numbers included many Jewish refugees fleeing persecution in Russia.

Few people traveled willingly to Ward's Island, but when she heard of the Jewish immigrants' plight, Emma Lazarus went there. She saw frightened people and heard stories of mass violence in their homeland. She went back to the island again and again, trying to understand what had happened to these people and what, if anything, she could do for them. Lazarus knew that the refugees' plight was made even worse because they were

Lazarus's handwritten copy of "The New Colossus," was auctioned in late 1883. The poem was relatively obscure until it was inscribed in bronze and placed on the pedestal of the Statue of Liberty 20 years later.

not really welcome in America. Their exodus from Russia had come at exactly the wrong time.

The United States had been built by immigrants, and throughout its history the U.S. government had actively encouraged people to come and settle in America. In the 1870s many American businesses sent representatives to Europe to convince people to emigrate and work in the booming factories of

A U.S. official checks newly arrived immigrants for obvious signs of illness. Although Lazarus could trace her family's history back to colonial America, she was deeply concerned with the immigrants' plight.

Russian refugees wait in one of New York's temporary housing stations. Fleeing anti-Semitic violence in their homeland, thousands of Russian Jewish immigrants arrived in New York during the early 1880s.

the Industrial Revolution. Underpopulated southern and western states sent out promotional brochures to attract European settlers, and land company agents lured peasants and farmers away from Scotland, Ireland, and Scandinavia.

In the 1880s, the United States still needed farmers and laborers to develop the vast North American continent, but some Americans felt that the Russian Jews could not make a productive contribution. Who were they, after all? Men and women who were weak with malnutrition, many of whom had never plowed a field or dug a ditch. Other Americans claimed that the new immigrants were bringing problems to the United States instead of contributing to its strength. Irish and Chinese immigrants, for instance, had provided the country with cheap labor to build railroads and mine coal, but now were blamed for creating city slums and spreading disease and crime. Other groups—such as the Italians, Poles, Hungarians, and Russian Jews—continued to stream into the United States and met with growing resentment as long-established Americans feared for their way of life.

In 1882, new laws entirely barred Chinese immigration and set quotas to restrict the number of new arrivals from several other countries. According to some Americans, the laws did not go far enough. They said it was time to close the country's doors. If that happened, Emma Lazarus knew that hundreds of thousands of people would be left to suffer and probably die in the old country.

This painful knowledge guided her thoughts as she worked on the sonnet that would help provide a pedestal for Bartholdi's sculpture. The statue itself was still in Paris, surrounded by scaffolding, and Lazarus had never seen it, but that did not matter. She had seen both the misery and hopefulness of America's immigrants, and that was enough to give her an idea. The poem she wrote that November day was called "The New Colossus," and it proclaimed:

Not like the brazen giant of Greek fame,
With conquering limbs astride from land
  to land;
Here at our sea-washed sunset gates
  shall stand
A mighty woman with a torch, whose
  flame
Is the imprisoned lightning, and her
  name
Mother of Exiles. From her beacon-hand
Glows world-wide welcome; her mild
  eyes command
The air-bridged harbor that twin cities
  frame.
"Keep, ancient lands, your storied
  pomp!" cries she
With silent lips. "Give me your tired,
  your poor,
Your huddled masses yearning to
  breathe free,

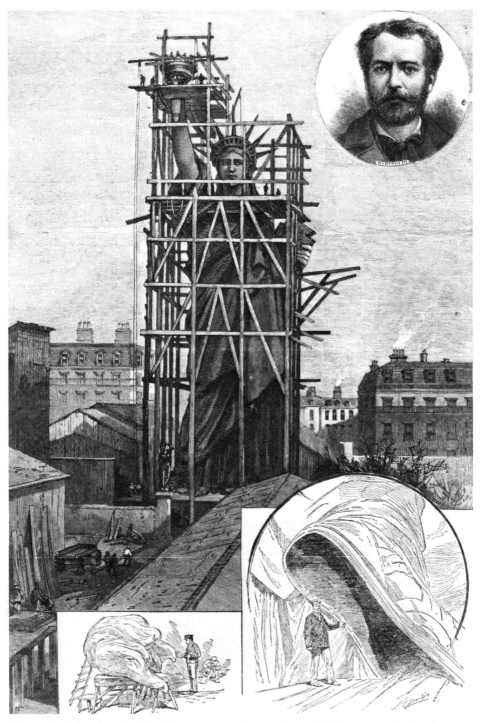

Liberty Enlightening the World *towers over the rooftops of 19th-century Paris, where the statue was erected before it was shipped to New York. French sculptor Frédéric-Auguste Bartholdi is shown in the upper right-hand corner.*

The wretched refuse of your teeming
  shore.
Send these, the homeless, tempest-tost
  to me.
I lift my lamp beside the golden door!"

Although Lazarus's poem and Frédéric-Auguste Bartholdi's sculpture have become inextricably linked in most people's minds, the two artists had very different views of "Lady Liberty." Bartholdi had designed an unyielding face that expressed victory over tyranny; Emma Lazarus envisioned features softened by human compassion. The sculptor sought to symbolize the alliance between two great powers, France and the United States; the poet described America's special meaning to oppressed people all over the world.

Emma Lazarus was famous, and so she could be confident that her verse would help raise money for the statue's pedestal. In that sense, her poem was sure to be a success. But her hopes for the sonnet were more ambitious than just raising money. She hoped it would help convince Americans that liberty would not be served if the U.S. government shut its doors to new arrivals, particularly to "less desirable" immigrants—the persecuted and impoverished victims of oppressive governments. But she was far from sure that her 12-line poem alone could get her point across. After all, it had taken Lazarus herself three decades to see the misery and injustice that existed beyond her own privileged life.

This 13th-century miniature shows a student learning Hebrew characters from a Jewish scholar. Initially indifferent to her religious background, Lazarus later wrote that their heritage imbued contemporary Jews with a "fiery pride."

T W O

"Fiery Pride"

In 19th-century America, many well-to-do families shielded their daughters from the realities of life, but Lazarus had been even more protected than most. Although she would spend much of her adult life championing the poor and the powerless, during her childhood and adolescence she knew little about the world outside the privileged and sheltered environment her parents created for her. Once, as a little girl, she saw her mother and father give money to the wife of a man who had been killed in an accident. Perplexed by their action, she asked them the reason for their charity. They told her that the woman was poor. Emma already had an extensive vocabulary, but this was the first time she had heard the word "poor."

She was born in Union Square, then one of New York City's most fashionable districts, on July 22, 1849. At the time of her birth, her parents, Moses and Esther Lazarus, already had three daughters, and a son and two more daughters soon followed. Moses Lazarus was a successful sugar merchant; his wife, true to 19th-century tradition, spent most of her time caring for the children and running the household. The family lived in a luxurious brownstone on West 14th Street, where they were attended by several servants.

New York City in the 19th century was a seaport town very different from the metropolis it is today. Most people lived and worked on the southern tip of Manhattan Island, where the horizon was broken by the masts and rigging of ships, not by the towering silhouettes of skyscrapers that now

Ferries and tugboats crowd the wharves of New York Harbor. The city was a bustling seaport in 1849, the year of Emma Lazarus's birth.

characterize the area. Engineers and architects had not yet devised the structural steel frames that make such tall buildings possible. The first passenger elevator would not be installed in New York until 1859, ten years after Emma's birth. Back in those days, "hailing a cab" meant flagging down a two-wheeled horse-drawn hansom, and "mass transit" referred to horse-carts with room for 25 to 30 passengers. There were no bright lights on Broadway or anywhere else. Homes and city streets were illuminated by oil-burning lamps.

At the time of Emma's birth, New York City's population was only 330,000. That number included 10,000 Jews, most of whom traced their history back to Spain and Portugal on the Iberian peninsula. They had descended from immigrants who had arrived in the New World as early as 1654, and called themselves Sephardim (or Sephardic Jews), from the Hebrew word for Spain. The Lazarus family was Sephardic, making them heirs to a tradition that, Emma Lazarus later wrote, gave her people a "fiery pride."

As a little girl, Emma's father told her about the triumphs—and sorrows—of

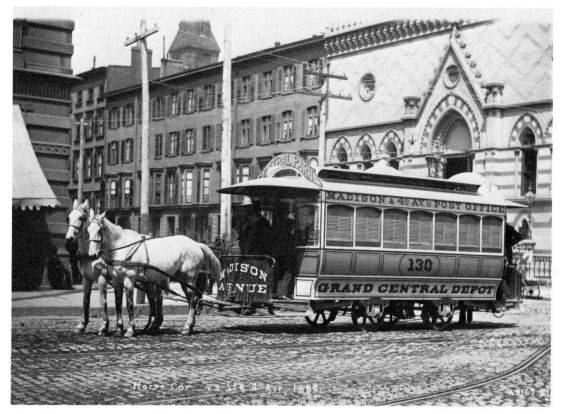

Horse-drawn carts provided New York City's mass transportation in the 19th century.

her family's illustrious ancestors. When most European Jews were being persecuted, the Sephardim were enjoying a Golden Age in Spain and Portugal, the countries that made up the Iberian peninsula. They were active in government, science, and literature. Their greatest era began in 711 A.D., following the Moorish conquest of the Iberian peninsula. For the next several centuries, while the rest of Europe was sunk in the primitive ignorance of the Middle Ages, the Moors, a Muslim people from northwest Africa, brought to Spain an advanced culture that em-

phasized learning and the arts. The Jews shared many of the Moors' values and rose to high positions in the realm.

Bit by bit, the original Christian European rulers of Spain and Portugal forced the Moors from the Iberian peninsula. Church leaders distrusted the Jews and coveted their wealth. Rumors began to fly, including claims that Jews used the blood of Christian infants for their religious rites. The situation worsened in 1270, when some Christian Europeans, frustrated by their inability to take the Holy Land from the Muslims during their last Crusade,

This 15th-century woodcut depicts Jews torturing a Christian child. Anti-Semitic propaganda flourished during the Middle Ages, and some rumored that Jews used the blood of Christian infants in their religious rituals.

turned their anger against non-Christians at home.

Riots broke out, and Sephardim were massacred by angry mobs. New restrictive laws were passed and many Jews and Muslims were forced to con-

vert to Christianity. Responding to this swelling tide of anti-Semitism, Spain's king and queen, Ferdinand and Isabella, launched the Inquisition in 1479. The Inquisition was a ruthless campaign led by the Catholic church to

Cross-wielding Catholic church officials menace Jewish prisoners during the Inquisition, an investigation into religious beliefs that was launched in 1479. The Inquisition quickly degenerated into a campaign against non-Christians; thousands of Jews were tortured and killed.

determine whether Jews who had converted were indeed devout Christians. Suspects accused of secretly observing Judaism were tortured to make them confess to their crime. If found guilty,

or if they were not sufficiently repentant, they were burned at the stake.

Ferdinand and Isabella finally issued the Expulsion Edict of 1492, which proclaimed: "We order all Jews and Jewesses of whatever age that before the end of this month of July they depart with their sons and daughters ... and not dare to return." The government of Portugal issued a similar declaration five years later.

Fourteen ninety-two also marked Columbus's discovery of the New World. Some of the Jews expelled from the Iberian peninsula eventually settled in South America. Though the Inquisition officially had authority over Spanish and Portuguese territories in the Americas, the colonies lay far from the center of power and were therefore relatively safe—provided the Sephardim were discreet about practicing their religion. In 1624, Holland conquered the Portuguese colony of Brazil, and in the next 30 years, thanks to Dutch tolerance, Jews began to observe their religion openly.

But in 1654 the Portuguese reconquered Brazil. The Jews, who by then had dropped all pretense of being Catholic, found themselves once more at the mercy of the Inquisition. The Sephardim escaped aboard 16 ships bound for Holland, then the most cosmopolitan—and tolerant—nation in Europe. But for 23 Jewish refugees, the real trouble was just about to begin.

A delegation of Jews asks Spain's monarchs, Ferdinand and Isabella, to repeal the Expulsion Edict of 1492. The monarchs did not relent, and all of the nation's Jews were driven from the country that same year.

On the high seas, their ship strayed during a storm and was captured by pirates who robbed the cargo, stripped the passengers of all their valuables, and planned to sell them into slavery. This fate was averted when a French ship battled the pirates and rescued the Jews. But when the captain, who had only assisted the ship because he expected a rich reward, found himself with nothing for his troubles but 23 frightened people, he angrily left them ashore at the tiny Dutch trading post of New Amsterdam, which later be-

came the English colony of New York. America's first Jews had landed.

The Lazarus family could trace its history back to that small group of 23 Sephardim. But during her childhood, Emma Lazarus, the heir to that distinctive tradition, was not concerned with her past. No one in her family had experienced anti-Semitism directly, and her parents were more interested in American society than in Jewish culture and history. She would later write that she was "brought up exclusively under American institutions,

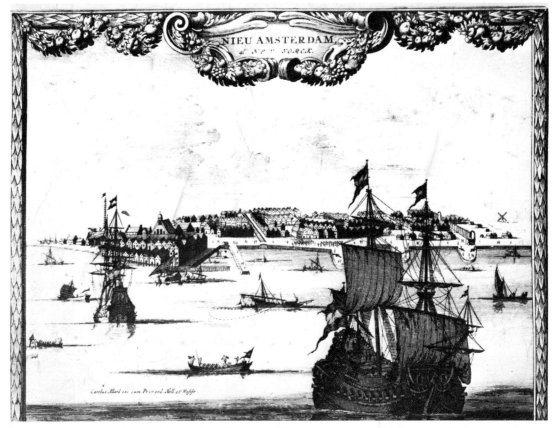

This early engraving shows the Dutch settlement of New Amsterdam, which eventually became New York. Lazarus was descended from America's first Jews, who arrived in the Dutch colony in 1654.

amid liberal influences, in a society where all differences of race and faith were fused in a refined cosmopolitanism." It was not until she reached adulthood that her heritage—and the dangers of anti-Semitism—became important to her.

At the age of six, Emma was examined by doctors who pronounced her too frail to attend school, and so she was educated at home by a tutor. Even when the family spent summers at their country home in Newport, Rhode Island, she was seldom allowed to venture outdoors. But although Emma was kept physically confined, she was encouraged in her intellectual explorations. She studied arithmetic, history, literature, and languages. She became fluent in French, German, and Italian. She learned to play the piano and soon became quite accomplished as a musician. Emma was a bright, serious, and occasionally somber little girl.

Emma was not only sheltered but

spoiled. During the Civil War, the period between 1861 and 1865 when the North and South fought over the issue of slavery, young Emma gave little thought to the men dying on battlefields and the freedom and rights of black Americans hanging in the balance. Instead, war shortages annoyed her. When 12-year-old Emma failed to receive the birthday present she wanted because of the shortages, she sulked and refused to say a word for the rest of the day.

In her isolation, Emma frequently escaped into fantasy—and literature. As her sister Josephine later remarked, "Books were her world from her earliest years. In them she literally lost and found herself." She loved the legends of King Arthur and his knights and sometimes pretended that her dolls were characters out of Arthurian lore—such as Queen Guinevere or Sir Lancelot. She admired her English-born tutor who gave her poetry to read and encouraged her to see American culture as primitive compared to that of Great Britain.

Emma's parents generally left her education up to her tutor, but when he introduced her to the works of England's greatest writer, William Shakespeare, Mrs. Lazarus was shocked. Like most women of her era, Esther Lazarus considered Shakespeare's poems and plays too violent and sexually explicit for a 13-year-old girl. The tutor was

Lazarus's parents considered the writings of 16th-century poet and playwright William Shakespeare too violent and sexually suggestive for their young daughter. The tutor who introduced her to Shakespeare's works was dismissed, and Moses Lazarus began to educate his daughter himself.

soon gone from the household, probably fired.

If Emma grieved at the loss, she forgot her sorrow when she found out who her new tutor would be. Her father had decided to retire from his business as a sugar merchant. He would stay home, devote himself to his family, and teach Emma himself.

Moses Lazarus was adored by his wife and seven children. The family was close-knit—perhaps too much so, according to Moses Lazarus's friend, antislavery activist Thomas Wentworth Higginson. He later described a visit to the Lazarus home: "I chanced to call at the house, and found everyone there in such distress that I thought something terrible must have occurred. My hasty inquiry of the daughters brought out the fact that their father was going away: But, I asked, he will come back? 'Yes, tomorrow night,' was the mournful reply." Clearly Moses Lazarus was more than the head of his household. To his wife and children, he seemed the center of the universe itself.

Now that he had decided to lavish his attention on teenage Emma and her education, they were together constantly. His original intention was to change the emphasis of Emma's studies on romantic literature, which her family suspected was contributing to her gloomy disposition. Her older sister Josephine characterized Emma's melodramatic nature as a "sign of youth, common especially among gifted persons whose sensibilities and imagination were not yet focused by reality." But Moses Lazarus, moved by his favorite daughter's passion for words, soon lost his resolve. He encouraged Emma not just to continue reading but to begin to write.

With her father's guidance, Emma immersed herself in the work of the great poets of Italy, Germany, and France. She read and translated verses by Petrarch, Johann Wolfgang von Goe-

the, Heinrich Heine, and Victor Hugo. She also wrote poetry about exotic places, heroism, ill-fated love, suffering, and death—things she knew nothing about from personal experience, but which she had spent countless days reading and dreaming about.

As the Civil War drew to a close in 1865, Emma had begun to understand the suffering that the bloody conflict had brought millions of Americans. She knew that the war had left many scars across the country, many of which would not be apparent until the fighting finally ceased. Her sensitivity was demonstrated in the opening stanza of a poem she wrote that year:

> More hearts will break than gladden when
> The bitter struggle's past;
> The giant form of Victory must
> A giant's shadow cast

President Abraham Lincoln was assassinated by John Wilkes Booth that same year. Emma, along with the rest of the nation, mourned, but while most writers expressed their grief and praised the slain leader, Emma took a more original approach and explored other emotions and ideas. In one poem, written very daringly from the point of view of the killer, she shows John Wilkes Booth searching without hope for a place to hide. Touched by Booth's burial in a secret, unmarked grave, Lazarus also wrote "The Mother's Prayer," in which Mrs. Booth says

Horse-drawn carts make their way down Manhattan's 14th Street in 1883. Lazarus grew up in a fashionable residential district a few blocks away.

John Wilkes Booth assassinated President Abraham Lincoln on April 14, 1865. Although Lazarus mourned the president's passing, she was intrigued by Booth and wrote two poems about him.

his daughter's poems were extraordinary and resolved to share her writings with other people. Putting together a collection of the work she had done between the ages of 14 and 16, he paid to have her writings published in 1867. Thirty-five original poems were included in the book, which was called *Poems and Translations*.

In those days, poetry was often published at the expense of the poet or the poet's family, so there was nothing unusual about Moses Lazarus footing the bill. What made the publication of Emma's work uncommon was that in the Victorian era respectable young girls and even grown women were not supposed to experience or express strong emotion. This notion discouraged many women from writing, while others published under masculine pen names.

Moses Lazarus resolved that, unlike many other women at the time, Emma would not have to hide her artistic talents in order to avoid public disapproval. He also thought that the book would never be sold to the public and would only be distributed among family members and friends. But Emma's verses aroused a great deal of interest, and the following year, *Poems and Translations* was reissued, this time for general circulation. One of the era's most respected poets, William Cullen Bryant, commented that Emma's poems were "better than any I remember

she will ". . . go to his victim's revered, honored tomb, And beg, of that merciful heart in the gloom" where she might find the body of her son.

Moses Lazarus was convinced that

to have seen written by any American girl of eighteen."

Emma was thrilled by the glowing public reception of her first book, but an even greater honor was in store for her. In December 1867, the young author and her father visited a banker named Samuel Gray Ward. Several other writers had been invited to Ward's gathering, but that evening was memorable for Emma because of the presence of one particular guest: Ralph Waldo Emerson, one of the most influential writers and philosophers in America. Overcoming her shyness, Emma approached Emerson and engaged him in conversation. Encouraged by his kindness and genuine interest in her ideas, she told him that she, too, had written a book. To her great joy, the philosopher asked her to send him a volume of her poetry. A stormy—but ultimately fruitful—relationship had begun.

Ralph Waldo Emerson, known as the "Sage of Concord," was a poet and essayist who preached individualism and communion with nature. Lazarus met him in 1867, and the two writers began a long correspondence.

THREE

The Sage of Concord

Ralph Waldo Emerson was a giant of his time. More than a poet and essayist who set new standards for American literature, he was also a philosopher who challenged the basic values and assumptions of American life. In Concord, Massachusetts, he had founded the Concord Group, a coterie of influential writers, including Henry David Thoreau and Nathaniel Hawthorne. The son of a minister, ordained as a minister himself, Emerson came to believe that harmony with nature could enrich the soul more than any church ritual. The Sage of Concord, as he was called, also spoke out against slavery and opposed the American stance in the Mexican War of the late 1840s, when the United States forced Mexico to cede Texas and sell the United States the territory that eventu-ally became New Mexico, Arizona, and California. Emerson enjoyed being provocative and was not afraid that his ideas might make him unpopular. In his essay "Self-Reliance," he urged people not to worry so much about public opinion. "Whoso would be a man," he wrote, "must be a non-conformist."

Emerson was 65 years old when 18-year-old Lazarus began to corre-spond with him. Even before their meeting, according to Lazarus's sister Josephine, his works were her "bread and wine." After he received her *Poems and Translations*, Emerson wrote to Lazarus, saying that her "poems have important merits." However, he was critical of the melancholy tone of many of the poems, remarking that Lazarus dwelled too much on life's "tragic and

U.S. troops land at Veracruz, Mexico, during the Mexican War of 1846–48. Unlike most Americans, Emerson openly opposed the war, which he condemned as reckless adventurism.

painful" aspects. Lazarus was not put off by his criticism; she saw that Emerson might be able to help her develop her craft. Years later, she would write about him: "To how many thousand youthful hearts has not his word been the beacon—nay, more, the guiding star—that leads them safely through periods of mental storm and struggle."

The Sage of Concord welcomed her letters warmly. "I should like to be your professor," he wrote her, "you being required to attend the whole term." Lazarus was only too happy to let the great man be her guide. Aside from advising her to avoid melodra-

matic themes, Emerson also recommended that she take up the study of Shakespeare that her worried mother had forbidden several years earlier. Shakespeare, he felt, would teach Lazarus to express her ideas clearly and succinctly.

She responded with long, frequent letters, turning to him as a mentor who would not only help her write poetry but also expand her horizons. Emerson encouraged the bookish young woman not to content herself with sensations filtered through literature, but to experience the world firsthand. "Books are a safe ground, and a long

Lazarus's letters to Emerson, which often contained her latest poems, were delivered to this house in Concord, Massachusetts, where he lived with his family.

one," he wrote, "but still introductory only...."

Lazarus took his advice to heart. She was vacationing with her family in Newport when she responded to Emerson's letter: "I am dismissing printed books ... because I have a nobler, vaster, more suggestive book lying all around me, with leaves ever open, inviting me to study and admire and love." Under his tutelage, she began, in her own words, "to see the light that plays upon the grass, to feel the mild breezes stir ... to gaze at the bright, breathing sea."

In one of his essays, Emerson had written, "The essence of friendship is entireness, a total magnanimity and trust." And that was what Lazarus wanted. She desperately wished that the Sage of Concord would be not only her professor but her devoted friend. Knowing that Emerson loved nature, Lazarus invited him to spend some time with her family at a house they had taken for the summer on Long Island Sound. "It is so beautiful ..." she wrote, "I do nothing but *look*, and am indolent enough not to think my time wasted." She made a vacation by the Sound seem very tempting, but Emerson declined the invitation.

Lazarus was disappointed that she would not see him again, but she knew she could still rely on his guidance and judgment. In her letters, she barraged him with questions about what she should read, what she should write, and how she should live her life.

At last Emerson, who had met her only once, warned her that he did not know her well enough to give her personal advice. "I am sorry to see," she wrote back, "that there is no forcing power to make friendship bud and bloom before years and experience have ripened it."

Lazarus looked forward to the day when the understanding between them would be deeper. In the meantime, she continued to send Emerson her work. She paid careful attention to his suggestions, whether he questioned her choice of a word or encouraged her to write about the world around her instead of remaining tied to Old World themes, subjects, and styles. Emerson had called for a poet "equal to our American possibilites," and Lazarus joined his crusade for a distinctive *American* culture. A few years after their correspondence began, she wrote a poem entitled "How Long," which urged American writers to break away from English influences:

How long, and yet how long,
Our leaders will we hail from over seas,
Masters and kings from feudal monar-
    chies,

And mock their ancient song
With echoes weak of foreign melodies?

That distant isle mist-wreathed,
Mantled in unimaginable green,
Too long hath been our mistress and
    our queen.
Our fathers have bequeathed
Too deep a love for her . . .

This fresh young world I see,
With heroes, cities, legends of her own;
With a new race of men, and overblown
By winds from sea to sea,
Decked with the majesty of every zone.

The distant siren-song
Of the green island in the eastern sea,
Is not the lay for this new chivalry,
It is not free and strong
To chant on prairies 'neath this brilliant
    sky.

The echo faints and fails;
It suiteth not, upon this western plain,
Our voice or spirit; we should stir again
The wilderness, and make the vales
Resound unto a yet unheard-of strain.

Although Lazarus was an enthusiastic protégée and able poet, Emerson's letters grew increasingly infrequent. In April 1870, he returned a long poem Lazarus had sent him unread, along with a note apologizing that he would not have time to read it. Lazarus was convinced that Emerson had tired of her and her letters and was no longer interested in her work.

In fact, Emerson was simply old and overworked. Some people even whispered that he was growing senile. He was often moody, and his life had been darkened by personal tragedy and loss.

But Lazarus knew nothing of this. To her, Emerson was the lofty Sage of Concord and she never guessed at the tumultuous human behind the facade of philosophical calm. All she knew was that her one connection to the outside world was fraying and might even break. Three months later, a worse blow was to fall.

Several published but largely unsubstantiated reports claim that Emma Lazarus had long had a passionate crush on her cousin, Washington Nathan, son of her favorite uncle, Benjamin. These accounts are certainly plausible, because Washington Nathan seemed to inspire intense feelings in almost every woman he met. Sporting a silk top hat over his wavy black hair and carrying a gold-handled walking stick, he was a familiar figure at New York's fashionable night spots. Gossip had it that no woman could resist a smile from his full lips or a glance from his blue eyes.

In 1870, Washington Nathan was 21 years old, the same age as Emma Lazarus. He, too, lived with his parents, but while his cousin was sheltered and overprotected, Washington Nathan led a wild life. According to rumor, he spent as much as $30,000 a year on liquor, clothes, fine food, and gifts for his many female admirers. His reputation grew worse all the time, but no one could have foreseen the terrible accusation he was soon to face. And

This drawing of Lazarus's uncle, Benjamin Nathan, accompanied a newspaper account that described his murder as "a mystery which puzzles our sharpest detectives."

whether Emma Lazarus was in love with her cousin or not, she would be deeply marked by what happened to the Nathan family in 1870.

The Nathans were spending the summer away from New York, but on the hot and humid day of July 28, Benjamin Nathan came back to town on business, along with Washington and one other son. Because it was the anniversary of his mother's death, Mr. Nathan decided to stay overnight in the city and attend synagogue services in the morning.

That evening, Washington Nathan and his brother went out for a night on the town. Their father drank a glass of ice water at about ten and went to sleep. In spite of the heat and humidity, the housekeeper locked all the doors and windows, as she did every night before retiring.

Benjamin Nathan was very proud that with the windows closed, his house was almost completely soundproof. No one inside was ever troubled by the racket of horses' hooves and carriage wheels in the street. Of course, no one passing by outside could hear any noise coming from within the house either. Later, people would testify that they had not heard any strange sounds at 12 West 23rd Street during the night of July 28. But something *did* happen.

The following morning Washington Nathan found his father lying in a doorway in a pool of blood, brutally bludgeoned to death. There were signs of a great struggle. A safe and a cashbox had been smashed open and their contents stolen. The police estimated that Mr. Nathan had been robbed and murdered between the hours of 2:00 and 3:00 in the morning.

Lazarus was shocked by the death of her favorite uncle and horrified when Washington Nathan was named one of the prime suspects in the murder.

Sensational accounts appeared in the press about Nathan's "loose living." Journalists implied that he might very well have killed his father in an argument over money. And if he had not, who could have done it? As speculation ran rampant, it seemed that the people of New York could talk of nothing else.

When Washington Nathan was questioned in court, his alibi created another scandal. A female acquaintance took the witness stand to testify that he had spent the night with her. In the end, for lack of evidence, no charges were ever brought against Washington Nathan. The case was never solved.

Emma Lazarus remained loyal to her cousin, convinced of his innocence. For his part, Washington Nathan inherited $75,000 from his father, squandered it all in riotous living, and became entangled in other scandals. Once while visiting an actress in her hotel, he was shot and wounded by a jealous woman. He quarreled with his heartbroken family and drifted away from them.

At the same time that her cousin's fortunes were fading, Emma Lazarus was winning new success and gaining public esteem. A match with Washington Nathan would not have been a happy one, and some biographers have speculated that Lazarus was referring to her frustrated infatuation with Nathan when she wrote of "de-

GST 20. 1870.] FRANK LESLIE'S ILLUSTRATED NEWSPAPER.

Washington Nathan is third from left in this sketch depicting the coroner's inquest into his father's murder. Lazarus's 21-year-old cousin was a prime suspect, but the case was never solved.

sires and yearnings that may find no rest," a "craving sense of emptiness and pain," and "grief to be conquered day by day." Whether she loved Na-

than or not, there is not even a hint that she ever fell in love with any other man.

Although distressed by the murder

ADMETUS

AND OTHER POEMS.

BY

EMMA LAZARUS.

NEW YORK:
PUBLISHED BY HURD AND HOUGHTON.
Cambridge: Riverside Press.
1871.

Emma Lazarus's second poetry anthology, Admetus and Other Poems, *was published in 1871. Lazarus dedicated the book "To my friend, Ralph Waldo Emerson."*

tently referred to himself as her tutor or professor, Lazarus dedicated the volume "To my friend, Ralph Waldo Emerson."

Emerson was not entirely comfortable with the dedication, but he was impressed by the poetry. In an enthusiastic letter, he exclaimed, "You have hid yourself from me until now, for the merits of the preceding poems did not unfold this fullness & high equality of power...." Lazarus also earned high praise from the *Illustrated London News*, a remarkable feat for an American poet. Some American critics were not as kind, but according to her sister Josephine, it almost did not matter to Lazarus what people said: No public praise was enough to satisfy Lazarus or put her insecurity at ease.

Despite her continued success, Lazarus longed for more reassurance, although it was not forthcoming from Emerson. In 1874 Emerson published *Parnassus*, an anthology of what he considered to be the best recent English and American poetry. Not a single verse by Lazarus was included. Filled with anger and self-pity, she wrote her famous mentor: "I felt as if I had won for myself by my own efforts a place in any collection of American poets, and I find myself treated with absolute contempt in the very quarter where I had been encouraged to build my fondest hopes. This public neglect is in such direct variance with the opinions you

of her uncle and the ensuing scandal, Lazarus never stopped writing, and in 1871 she published her second book, a collection of poetry called *Admetus and Other Poems*. The title poem, "Admetus," was based on a Greek myth about a woman who gave up her life to save her husband. She dedicated the book to Emerson. Though he consis-

Lazarus enjoyed the writings of Edgar Allan Poe, author of such melancholy tales of the supernatural as "The Raven." Her early writings were often somber pieces in which Poe's influence was evident.

The works of 19th-century German composer Robert Schumann were special favorites of Emma Lazarus. In the 1870s, she composed several sonnets based on his lushly romantic music.

have expressed to me in private, that it leaves me in utter bewilderment as to your real verdict...."

Emma Lazarus had always had a somewhat melancholy outlook, and her sister Josephine said she was even morbid. As a girl, she had loved the eerie, gloomy tales and poems of Edgar Allan Poe, and when she sat down to play the piano she often chose something sorrowful and romantic by Schu-mann or Chopin. This predisposition, coupled with Emerson's seeming dismissal of her talent, drove Lazarus into a deep depression. The bright, ambitious, and energetic side of her personality was overwhelmed by a profound sadness. She lost the desire or ability to speak and simply sat one day after another. Her depression deepened into a condition that might today be called a nervous breakdown.

Johann Wolfgang von Goethe was the inspiration for Lazarus's first novel, Alide. The book presented an idealized view of the German poet, whom she felt had the right to betray his lover in the name of art.

FOUR

Explorations

Emma Lazarus sat at home, overcome by the sort of strong emotion that had always fascinated her. At some point, though, during the days and weeks of inner turmoil, she underwent a change. In his very first letter to her years earlier, Ralph Waldo Emerson had declared that "grief, passion, disaster are only materials of Art." Now, Lazarus began to write about her feelings.

Before her breakdown, she had begun a novel based on the youthful romance between the great German writer Johann Wolfgang von Goethe and a woman he had fallen in love with and later abandoned. Now the idea resurfaced as she emerged from her bleak trance. All of her own pain poured onto the page as she recreated the feelings of Goethe's abandoned lover. By the time the book, *Alide*, was finished at the end of 1874, its author had recovered from her depression. *Alide* was a critical success, and the prominent Russian novelist Ivan Turgenev wrote Lazarus to tell her that her "characters are drawn with a pencil as delicate as it is strong." Proud of her success, Lazarus was ready to face life again.

Two years after the publication of her first novel, she received a surprising invitation from Ralph Waldo Emerson. After she had sent him her angry letter when she discovered that she had been left out of the *Parnassus* anthology, she had not expected to hear from her mentor again. But now, the Sage of Concord was asking her to travel up to Massachusetts and spend a brief vacation at his home.

Lazarus was not sure whether Emerson had forgiven her outburst or had merely forgotten it. According to gossip, his memory was so bad by the 1870s (when Emerson was in his seventies) that his lectures were disorganized and full of mistakes. Some scholars have suggested that when Emerson made his selections for *Parnassus* he had been suffering from mental distraction, and that was why he had neglected to include works by Lazarus and two other contemporary poets of even greater renown: Walt Whitman and Edgar Allan Poe.

Lazarus decided to put the past behind her. She was thrilled at the prospect of the trip; Emerson was, at last, treating her as a real friend. And she was pleased with the prospect that she might meet interesting people. Emerson's home had long been a center of American intellectual life.

Emerson and some of the other writers of the Concord Group had been closely connected with the Transcendentalist movement that flourished in New England in the 1830s and 1840s. The Transcendentalists had tried to break away from the severe heritage of New England Puritanism while preserving its idealism and sense of mission: They pursued "plain living and high thinking." Some members of the group lived in small communities structured around their ideals; others were also closely identified with the abolitionist cause, which called for an end to slavery.

Many of the Transcendentalists experimented in group living at a commune called Brook Farm. Later, Amos Bronson Alcott, the father of author Louisa May Alcott, with his family and a few associates formed the Fruitlands commune. There, a typical meal consisted of apples washed down with cold water, and residents refused to wear cotton clothing to avoid buying the main product of the slave-owning South. One member of the community suggested dispensing with clothes altogether. He was overruled but was known to slip off occasionally and wander around naked in the woods at night.

Emerson kept his distance from this kind of social experimentation, but his home did become a frequent meeting place for the group. From 1842 to 1844, he also edited the Transcendentalist magazine, *The Dial*, which presented new literary work as well as controversial articles such as essays on women's rights written by social critic and reformer Margaret Fuller.

Transcendentalism as an organized movement had faded by 1845, but its influence—especially its emphasis on individual morality—can be seen in almost every counterculture movement in America since then, even those of the mid- and late 20th century. As Emma Lazarus headed for Concord in

1876, she knew that members of the group still lived in the area and she might have the chance to meet them.

When she boarded the train, in August 1876, Lazarus had earned the right to be taken seriously as one of the most creative minds of her era. She had published three books, and her poems had appeared in prestigious magazines both in America and abroad. After years of isolation from the world, she had carved out a place for herself at the center of American intellectual life. But though she was 27 years old, she had never before been away from her family, not even for a single day.

Her visit to Concord did not get off to a good start. In keeping with his belief that the simple life is best, Emerson met Lazarus at the station in a modest little cart, drawn by a single horse. At first sight, the 73-year-old, white-haired poet matched the image of Emerson that Lazarus had cherished for so long. She was eager to engage him in deep discussion, but she was in for a few surprises.

She had hardly arrived when the Emersons decided to retire for the

Emerson, standing at center, lectures on philosophy in a Concord classroom. A leader of the Transcendentalist movement of the 1830s and 1840s, he was still an influential man of letters in the last years of his life, when Lazarus knew him.

Amos Bronson Alcott, the father of author
Louisa May Alcott, attempted to apply the
Transcendentalists' philosophy of "plain living
and high thinking" at a commune called
Fruitlands.

Lazarus woke up the next morning anxious to resume their conversation, but learned that Emerson could not be disturbed. She stationed herself on the threshold of his study and stayed there for hours, but Emerson did not emerge. Even though he no longer worked very much, he still had the habit of secluding himself for most of the day to think his own thoughts.

After this reception, Lazarus realized that her hero had not invited her to Concord to get to know her better. Instead, he had meant for her to be a companion to his daughter, Ellen.

Her disappointment was soon tempered when she discovered that she did not like Emerson so much after all. Though he had given up the pulpit, he was still a preacher at heart and in style and did not seem to know how to carry on a casual conversation. As the days passed, Lazarus found herself increasingly annoyed with his pompous manner. After years of trying to win this man's approval and personal regard, she began to wonder whether she really wanted to be friends with him at all. He did not even care for music, and Lazarus did not see how any sensitive person could live in this world and not love Chopin. For years, she had lived by Emerson's judgments, and now it turned out that he was not perfect after all. In many respects, her disillusionment with Emerson was liberating. Lazarus would never again feel

night. Lazarus, however, convinced Emerson to let her sit with him for a while in his study. The great man agreed reluctantly, having grown rather antisocial in his old age and wary by now of his protégée's demands. To his relief and her delight, they thoroughly enjoyed their hour and a half of talk.

Emerson spent most of his time in this study, a refuge from the outside world where he could be alone with his thoughts. During her visit to Concord, Lazarus was dismayed when she was not admitted to the poet's sanctum.

as though her entire worth depended on the opinion of one man.

Although disappointed with her former mentor, Lazarus grew to enjoy the company of Emerson's wife and daughter, whom she later described as "the stately, white-haired Mrs. Emerson, and the beautiful, faithful Ellen."

Emerson (standing in back row) joins his family for this 1879 portrait. Lazarus became disillusioned with her mentor during her stay at his home, but she grew quite close to his wife and daughter Ellen.

Lazarus had lost her own mother two years earlier, and Mrs. Emerson's warmth and kindness helped her get over her loss. Ellen Emerson, who had taught Protestant Sunday school, later recalled how amazed she had been to meet "a real unconverted Jew." She later remarked that their discussions about religion were "more interesting than I could have imagined," and that Lazarus was "a pleasant—if somewhat intense!—companion." The two young women soon became close friends.

Lazarus also befriended another person during her stay in Concord: William Ellery Channing, a Transcendentalist who had written a biography of Henry David Thoreau. A poet who had contributed to *The Dial*, Channing had in his youth been encouraged by Emerson just as Lazarus had—except that he had been a young poet before Lazarus was even born. In his old age, he had trouble getting along with most people. "Generally crabbed and reticent with strangers," Lazarus recalled in her journal, "he took a liking to me. The bond of our sympathy was my admiration for Thoreau, whose memory he actually worships. . ."

The two poets talked for hours on end about Henry David Thoreau, another contributor to *The Dial*, and nonconformist member of the Concord Group. Thoreau is often considered the father of American civil disobedience—political protest, the nonviolent refusal to obey the law. He was a conductor on the Underground Railroad that illegally helped slaves escape to freedom, and he once spent the night in jail rather than pay taxes to a government that tolerated the institution of slavery. Believing that "a man is rich in proportion to the number of things he can afford to let alone," Thoreau sought to strip his needs down to the barest essentials. In 1845, he built a simple hut by Walden Pond, on property belonging to Emerson, and lived there alone.

Contrary to popular understanding, Thoreau did not wish or claim to give up all contact with people. He continued to see his family and friends and join them for dinner, and many visitors came out to Walden Pond to see the primitive hut and, if possible, to catch a glimpse or exchange a few words with its strange inhabitant. Thoreau liked living this way because in only about six weeks of work as a surveyor, carpenter, fence builder, or other

Transcendentalist poet William Ellery Channing became fond of Lazarus during her Concord visit. "Generally crabbed and reticent with strangers," Lazarus reported, "he took a liking to me."

skilled laborer he could earn enough money to meet his expenses for the entire year. That left him plenty of time for what he thought more important than the ordinary task of earning a living. He was able to devote himself to writing, thinking, and enjoying the beauties of nature. *Walden*, the account he wrote of his stay by Emerson's pond, became an American

Lazarus admired the individualistic philosophy of Henry David Thoreau, who wrote, "If a man does not keep pace with his companions, perhaps it is because he hears a different drummer. Let him step to the music he hears, however measured or far away."

beauty. So strong, in fact, was her feeling that it frightened her a little. "My tastes tend toward solitude as it is," she once wrote to Emerson. If she let herself indulge in her enjoyment of nature as much as she desired, she feared she would become "a permanent savage."

But with Channing by her side, telling stories about Thoreau, she happily wandered past streams and trees or sat in silence, contemplating the colors of the sky. Lazarus later described their experience in idyllic terms: "I sat with him in the sunlit wood, looking at the gorgeous blue and silver summer sky." They went to see a pile of stones by Walden Pond that was all that remained of Thoreau's hut. The man himself had died in 1862, without seeing the end of slavery, and 14 years later, Channing still could not acknowledge his friend's death. As Lazarus recorded in her journal, he never allowed himself to say "When he died," but rather said "When Mr. Thoreau went away from Concord," as though he was merely out of town and might return any day. And though Channing willingly took Lazarus along on walks through the Concord forests and hills, he couldn't keep from telling her, "None of it looks the same as when I looked at it with him."

classic. In his book, he urged his readers to "live deeply and suck out all the marrow of life."

This lesson was not lost on Lazarus, who was shedding the shyness and awkwardness that had come from her sheltered early life. She also understood Thoreau's impulse to escape social restrictions, and she, too, had a strong emotional response to natural

Lazarus clearly made a deep impression on Channing. When she left Concord to return home, he gave her one

A pile of stones was all that remained of Thoreau's hut at Walden Pond when Lazarus visited the site in 1876, 14 years after the philosopher's death.

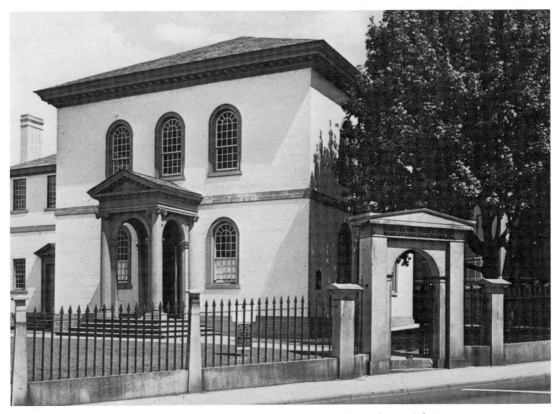

Rhode Island's 18th-century Touro Synagogue was the subject of "In the Jewish Synagogue at Newport," Lazarus's first poem to draw on her Jewish ancestry.

of his most treasured possessions, the pocket compass that Thoreau had always carried when exploring the woods. Back in New York, Lazarus resumed a warm and friendly correspondence with Emerson and his daughter. Though she no longer idolized Emerson, she was glad to have him as a friend, and she still kept his picture on her mantelpiece.

These were happy and productive days. The Lazaruses prepared to move uptown to East 57th Street, yet another fashionable neighborhood. Her work was being published in some of the nation's major magazines, while in New York, the Jewish community looked on her with special pride.

The only threat to her well-being came when Moses Lazarus fell ill in the autumn of 1876. His daughter had, it seems, given up all thoughts of marriage. If she had to devote herself to any man—and women in her day did not live on their own—she was content for that man to be her adored father. But with his illness, she was forced to realize that she might lose him. Her meeting with Channing had shown her how bleak life can appear when a loved one dies.

By November, Mr. Lazarus had recovered, but his daughter remained shaken. "There can be no freedom from anxiety about him night or day in future . . . ," she wrote, "but I try to shut my eyes resolutely to the yesterdays and tomorrows."

Although outwardly Lazarus seemed an exceptionally dutiful daughter, some biographers have theorized that a play she wrote that same year, *The Spagnoletto* (*The Little Spaniard*), vented some of the misgivings that Lazarus had about her relationship with her father. The verse drama, a tragedy set in 17th-century Italy, told the story of a painter who loves his daughter so much that he keeps her locked up at home. The naive daughter runs away with a nobleman who eventually deserts her. By the play's end, the father commits suicide in his daughter's presence, punishing her for deserting him.

Whether or not *The Spagnoletto* reflected Lazarus's feelings about her father, the play was so melodramatic and grim that it was never published or produced on stage. A modern critic, Dan Vogel, wrote that "All the charac-

ters in her play are set, posed, wooden, and unidimensional. *The Spagnoletto* leaps from extreme mood to extreme mood without realism or gradation." Lazarus was well aware of the play's shortcomings and suspected that the problem lay in her choice of subject matter. For the next two years she cast about for different topics to write on. Many of her poems were published in leading magazines, but Lazarus was still dissatisfied with her work.

One day in 1878, Edmund Clarence Stedman, a well-known poet and critic, suggested that Lazarus draw on her own heritage as a Jew for her writings. Lazarus was hesitant; she had always felt more American than Jewish. But Jewish history had touched a chord in her; more than 10 years earlier she had written her first poem on a Jewish theme, called "In the Jewish Synagogue at Newport." The verse was inspired by a trip she took to Touro Synagogue, built in Newport, Rhode Island, by Sephardic Jews in 1763. The builders had equipped the structure with a trap door and a tunnel as a symbolic reminder of their past as "secret Jews." Since the time of the publication of "In the Jewish Synagogue at Newport," she had returned to traditional themes and been dissatisfied with the results. By the late 1870s, as she searched for a new theme, Lazarus discovered instead an old one: the history of her people.

Russian Jewish immigrants salute the welcoming figure of the Statue of Liberty in this 1892 engraving. Lazarus had become involved in the refugees' cause a decade earlier, before the statue was erected in New York Harbor.

FIVE

"The Tempest-Tost"

Gustav Gottheil, the rabbi of New York City's Temple Emanu-El, was a man with a mission: He wanted to revitalize New York's Jewish community. When he arrived in the United States from Germany, he saw that the religious convictions of many American Jews had weakened as they assimilated into American culture. Gottheil's goal was to reverse this trend. As he became acquainted with the Lazarus family, he was convinced that he might be able to bring them back into the fold.

The Lazaruses had some interest in Jewish history, but they, like so many others, failed to observe Jewish law. They remained members of the congregation at the historic synagogue, Shearith Israel, but they rarely, if ever, attended services. For years they had not fasted, as required, on the solemn Day of Atonement. And although Jewish law prohibited the eating of pork and shellfish, the Lazaruses often had ham on the breakfast table, and during summer vacations at Newport, Rhode Island, a favorite pastime had always been digging and eating the delicious local clams.

Still, Rabbi Gottheil was not discouraged by their casual religious attitudes. He was especially interested in Emma Lazarus, because he felt that her fame might make her a role model for other Jewish women. He was determined to win her back to Jewish ways, not by arguing with her or challenging her, but by encouraging her reawakening interest in her heritage. He gave her medieval Hebrew poetry to read and translate and encouraged her to study

Victims of bubonic plague awaiting medical attention are depicted in this 15th-century painting. Lazarus's drama The Dance to Death, *chronicled the persecution of the Jews of the Middle Ages, who served as scapegoats as the plague—and panic—spread across Europe.*

the history of her people. Gottheil also asked Lazarus to translate some traditional Jewish hymns—and to write some new ones.

Lazarus was no longer the impressionable young woman anxious for a wiser, older mind to guide her life. Now she made it clear that she had her own principles. "I will gladly assist you as far as I can," she offered politely, "but that will not be much. I shall always be loyal to my race, but I feel no religious fervor in my soul." She pointed out that she probably lacked the kind of belief and enthusiasm that a good translator of prayers and hymns would need.

For the next four years, she would find inspiration in Jewish themes and would work on projects at Rabbi Gottheil's request, all the while remaining committed to a philosophy based on ethics rather than on the worship of God. And all the while, Rabbi Gottheil would continue his quiet campaign to win her back to the Jewish way of life.

Inspired by her newfound awareness of Jewish history, Lazarus wrote a powerful drama in verse, *The Dance to Death*. The play was based on accounts of the widespread slaughter of European Jews in the Middle Ages who were blamed for the spread of the bubonic plague. As panic spread along with the deadly disease, thousands of Jews were burned to death. In Lazarus's play, one of the victims of the hysteria gives an impassioned speech before he dies, telling his fellow Jews not to despair, for future generations of Jews will no longer be victims of prejudice:

> Ours is the truth,
> Ours is the power, the gift of Heaven.
>   We hold
> His Law, His lamp, His covenant, His
>   pledge.
> Wherever in the ages shall arise
> Jew-priest, Jew-poet, Jew-singer, or Jew-
>   saint—
> And everywhere I see them star the
>   gloom—
> In each of these the martyrs are
>   avenged!

Lazarus's *Dance to Death* ended on a positive note, as the victims looked forward to a future in which the Jewish people would not become scapegoats whenever other groups felt threatened. But even as Lazarus was writing this drama, history was repeating itself in faraway Russia.

In the second half of the 19th century, Russia's leader, Czar Alexander II, embarked on a series of social reforms that included liberating the nation's serfs (farm laborers forced to work for wealthy landowners). The country was in an uproar. Russia's upper classes, fearful that they would lose their wealth and power, did all they could to undermine the czar and his liberalization program. At the same time, radicals who called themselves "nihilists" insisted that the czar's initiatives had not gone far enough, pointing out that the recently freed serfs were still gripped by poverty. They argued that the Russian system was so rotten that it could not be reformed from within, but only through the use of revolutionary terror.

A group of nihilist conspirators, calling themselves The People's Will, made several attempts to assassinate the czar. They finally succeeded in March 1881. The slain czar's son rose to the throne as Alexander III and his government began to round up the conspirators. Unfortunately for the Jews who lived within the borders of the Russian Empire, two of the arrested members of The People's Will turned out to be Jewish.

Suddenly, the Jews as a group were blamed for Alexander II's murder. Rumors also began to fly that the Jews,

Czar Alexander II was a reform-minded ruler beloved by many Russians, including most Jews. His 1881 assassination sparked anti-Semitic riots, called pogroms, when it was revealed that two of the men involved in his murder were Jews.

Elisavetgrad on April 27. A Jewish inn-keeper and a drunken peasant got involved in an argument that became a fistfight. The violence escalated, and several people were badly hurt when men began attacking Jews all over the town. A week later, a Jewish delegation from Kiev went to see that city's governor-general. They had heard rumors that mob violence was about to break out against them, and they hoped the government would send troops to protect them and put down any trouble. General Drenteln's answer showed how much help they could expect: "I cannot endanger the lives of my soldiers," he said, "for the sake of a few Jews."

He did not relent. The police and military forces stood by, refusing to intervene, while a rampaging crowd stormed through the section of the city where the Jews were required to live. The mob burned and looted homes and stores and set the pattern of wanton destruction, murder, and rape that was to be repeated in more than 150 Russian towns by the year's end.

Worse, it soon became clear that the terrible riots, called pogroms, were not spontaneous outbursts, but were actually being organized by Russians with power and money. The pogroms always seemed to occur immediately following the appearance of strangers in town who carried lots of money and talked about "the Jewish conspiracy,"

not the upper classes, were responsible for the continuing economic misery of the former serfs. Once again, threatened people transformed their fear, rage, and helplessness into anti-Semitic violence.

Rioting first broke out in the town of

Pursued by club-wielding Christians, Jews flee from a Russian village. In 1881, the London Times *called Russia the "scene of horrors that have hitherto only been perpetrated in medieval days during times of war."*

This 1881 cartoon entitled "Live and Let Live in Russia" shows a Russian whipping a Jewish man. The caption reads, "Your money, Jew, or your life."

while they bought drinks for the local peasants. Their task was done when they had worked the peasants into a drunken, murderous rage.

Though it has not been established that the Russian imperial government was directly involved, Alexander III responded to the pogroms with anti-Semitic statements, and no one in authority took any steps to protect the Jews.

Instead, in May 1882, the czar an-nounced new laws aimed against the Jews. They were stripped of their land, forbidden to live in any rural areas, and confined to designated towns. There, without work, and isolated from the agricultural food-producing re-gions of the country, death came through starvation and through the diseases that spread in the over-crowded, unsanitary towns. A leading official of the Russian Orthodox Church was reported to say there was

Persecuted Russian Jews flee their homeland to travel westward across Europe. Once they reached England, thousands of Jewish refugees sailed to America in the hopes of starting new lives.

a three-point plan to deal with Russia's Jews: let one-third of them die, force one-third to emigrate, and make the rest convert.

The Jews were only too willing to cooperate with the second part of the plan. By the hundreds of thousands, they kept streaming toward the border, desperate to leave the land where they had been born.

News of the atrocities spread to the rest of Europe, then to America. In New York, a committee headed by former president Ulysses S. Grant hosted a meeting on the plight of Russia's Jews. William Evarts, the politician who would later ask Lazarus to compose the poem that became "The New Colossus," personally invited Lazarus to attend the meeting. Evarts gave a moving speech, in which he pointed out that sympathetic Americans had a duty toward their fellow human beings overseas: "It is not that it is the oppression of Jews by Russia: it is that it is the oppression of men and women by men and women; and we are men and women."

One group of refugees made a direct appeal to Americans: "Give us a chance in your great and glorious land of liberty, whose broad and trackless acres offer an asylum and a place for weary hearts. . . ." As she learned more about the refugees' suffering and witnessed their desperation and hopefulness with her own eyes, Emma Lazarus would make the refugees' appeal her own. She would transform their cries into poetry—poetry that touched the heart and, more importantly, shaped public opinion.

Gustav Gottheil, the rabbi of New York's historic Temple Emanu-El (pictured here), took Lazarus on her first trip to Ward's Island—an experience that changed her life. Before this, according to her sister Josephine, "Judaism had been a dead letter to her."

SIX

The Promised Land

There was no United Nations back in 1882, and most prosperous countries of the world did not feel obliged to assist the thousands of Jewish refugees who had escaped Russia's pogroms and faced uncertain futures. Many European leaders felt their generosity need go no further than allowing the fleeing Jews to cross their borders. As far as real assistance was concerned, it was up to the Jewish community to take care of its own.

Groups such as the Alliance Israélite stepped in to do the job. A worldwide Jewish federation founded in 1860 and based in France, the alliance was dedicated to the idea that well-to-do Jews should aid Jews in distress. Relying on contributions from members all over Europe, the group helped find new homes for the refugees and even paid their travel costs.

Month after month, thousands of Jews poured out of Russia, headed for points west. Those who had been poor all their lives were joined by those who were recently impoverished by the czar's policies and the necessity of fleeing their homeland with little more than the clothes on their backs. Formerly prosperous men and women found themselves sleeping on the ground and taking their meals in charity kitchens. Some of the more fortunate refugees used their small savings to purchase their passage to Europe and America, while others waited in overcrowded camps, hoping for assistance that would enable them to set up new lives.

Russian refugees eat a simple meal of soup and bread at a temporary shelter in London. The author of the article that accompanied this drawing called these exiles the "poor relations" of western Jews.

As they traveled westward, the refugees were often greeted at stops along the way by Jews, who offered them tea, rolls, or occasionally a real meal of soup or meat. In major cities such as Berlin, Germany, wealthy aristocrats donated some of their discarded finery. These acts of charity created some strange scenes and bizarre contrasts: An old man wearing the long beard and frayed black caftan of an Old Testament patriarch sported the highly polished, pointed shoes of a dandy; women in patched and dirty garments wore fashionable new hats topped with huge ostrich plumes.

Many of the refugees did not know where they would go or what the future would bring, but they could already envision a better life. The European Jews who came to meet them once they crossed Russia's borders seemed to be happy and confident people. The refugees began to glimpse

The exotic appearance of these newly arrived Russian immigrants creates a stir on the streets of New York. Some American Jews feared that the influx of Russian Jews would contribute to anti-Semitism.

a world they had never experienced or seen before. Apparently there were places where Jews were treated like everyone else, where the government was a friend, not an oppressor. Some of the Russian Jews remained in European cities along the route westward, but most descended on the English port of Liverpool to board ships bound for the United States. America was their dream.

There was only one catch: America did not want them. In recent years, the northern European Protestant majority had begun to feel threatened by the influx of Catholic and Jewish immigrants from southern and eastern Europe. Some Americans felt that the

nation was changing too much, too fast. Although most Americans were sympathetic to the plight of the Russian refugees, many did not want them to settle in the United States; they wanted to close America's doors to those who were not of similar backgrounds.

Some Jewish Americans were no more anxious than the Protestants to see the refugees come to American shores. In spite of their shared religion, they did not identify with the Russian Jews. The Russians' old-fashioned religious fervor seemed out of place in the new industrial world.

But more than anything else, the American Jews were frightened. They

70

knew that the recent growth of the Jewish population had contributed to an increase in anti-Semitism, mostly aroused by Jews who did not blend into the dominant Protestant culture. The arrival of thousands of ragged and hungry Russian Jews, uneducated except in religious matters and ill-equipped for American life, seemed guaranteed to stir up more prejudice.

In spite of delays, misunderstandings, ill will, and fears, more than 25,000 Jewish men, women, and children arrived in the United States by the end of 1882. Many of them were sent to rural areas such as South Dakota and Louisiana where they struggled—usually unsuccessfully—to become farmers. Others moved into cheap lodgings near the emigration depot of Castle Garden in New York and found work. Hundreds of others were housed in temporary shelters built on Ward's Island after the German-Jewish financier Jacob Schiff contributed $10,000 to build barracks for the refugees.

German-born Jewish immigrants, known as Ashkenazim, were the most active in the resettlement efforts, contributing money to feed, clothe, and

Immigrants eat a meal provided for them by the U.S. government. National agencies and private donations fed and sheltered newly arrived immigrants but seldom eased their transition to life in the New World.

71

This drawing shows Castle Garden, a station for processing immigrants after their arrival in America. In 1892, Castle Garden was closed and replaced by a larger immigrant depot, Ellis Island.

house the refugees. Perhaps they remembered their own experiences as new arrivals in America not that long before. The long-established Sephardic Jews hardly participated at all. An exception was Emma Lazarus, who became involved in the relief program through her friendship with Rabbi Gottheil. It was he who convinced her to visit the crowded refugee camp on Ward's Island.

Her eyes were opened by the suffer-ing she witnessed there, and Lazarus returned again and again. She went not only to Ward's Island, but to the tiny, overcrowded city apartments that some of the immigrants had moved into. She brought them food and clothing, and befriended some of the recent arrivals. After meeting one young student who was using the contributions of American Jews to be educated at an American university, she decided to support his cause. She enclosed a con-

72

A Russian observes the Jewish Sabbath in his first home in America, a coal cellar on Manhattan's Lower East Side. Many Jewish immigrants settled in this neighborhood after they left temporary shelters such as Ward's Island.

tribution in a letter to Rabbi Gottheil which insisted, "I wish you would please impress it very emphatically upon his mind that I do not wish it to be known *to anyone but himself* how I have befriended him."

Her trips to the island were painful ones. Emma Lazarus was shy with strangers under the best of circum-stances. Confronted with people un-like any she had ever known, it is no wonder she was often uncomfortable and stiff with the immigrants she meant to help. One of them, Abraham Cahan, who went on to become an important writer and editor, wrote about her in later years with a touch of bitterness. He remembered Lazarus as

a "wealthy young Jewish lady who belonged to the cream of monied aristocracy." He also sarcastically noted that her frequent visits with the poorest members of America's underclass "never undermined her status as an aristocrat."

Indeed, in spite of her sympathies and good works, Emma Lazarus was still every inch the proper young woman from genteel New York society. She spent most of her time aiding the new immigrants, but she seldom felt at ease with them. When she visited Ward's Island, she felt most comfortable with the intellectuals among the refugee population, whom she described as "men of brilliant talents and accomplishments, the graduates of Russian universities. . . ."

Although her awkwardness in dealing directly with the new immigrants could easily have been mistaken for haughtiness, there was no mistaking her zeal for the refugees' cause, which quickly found expression in her writing. Her first public defense of the Russian immigrants came in 1882.

For several years, Lazarus had contributed to the widely read and respected *Century* magazine. The editor,

Homeless immigrant children sleep on a New York City street. Sympathy for the immigrants moved Lazarus to provide them with practical assistance—and infused her writing with a new fervor.

After his arrival in America, writer Abraham Cahan met Lazarus when she visited Ward's Island. Mistaking her awkwardness for arrogance, he later charged that Lazarus had a patronizing attitude toward the new immigrants.

Richard Watson Gilder, was a friend of hers. Apparently it was Gilder who handed her an advance copy of the April 1882 issue, saying, "Here's something you'll be surprised at."

As she thumbed through the pages of *Century*, she found an article written by an important Russian scholar on the subject of the recent pogroms.

Zinaida Alexievna Ragozin's "Russian Jews and Gentiles" maintained that the Russian Jews had brought the violence upon themselves. If one looked at the riots from a "historical perspective," she claimed, they were nothing but a "spontaneous outburst of popular rage." The Jews, she wrote, had earned Christian Russia's distrust. Ragozin claimed that many of the Jews were "worshippers of the Golden Calf" who cared only for money—which they obtained by cheating the Russian people. She also accused the Jews of conspiring with an underground network of foreign Jews to destroy Russia. Ragozin was an internationally known historian; anything she wrote had to be taken seriously. An outraged Emma Lazarus certainly took Ragozin's article seriously.

Emma Lazarus could hardly believe what she was reading. For the first time, she realized that there were people in the world who simply hated all Jews, whether American, Russian, rich, or poor. Whatever her own achievements, whatever her family's social distinction, such people would hate her, too.

Suddenly, the Russian refugees no longer seemed alien. She could relate to them as her sisters and brothers. Helping them was no longer a simple charitable undertaking. Lazarus could at last imagine herself in their place and see that their cause was her own.

The *Century* article was an outrage. Gilder had a policy of encouraging free speech and never censoring opinions, but still, how could he have published such inflammatory lies? At the bottom of the Ragozin piece, an editor's note stated that the charges seemed "medieval" and that a reply to them would appear in the next issue. That, at least, was a good sign, though a lot would depend on who wrote the reply. It would have to be someone as articulate and well-respected as the Russian historian, someone tough enough to confront anti-Semitism and yet diplomatic enough not to offend ordinary readers.

The Gilders kept an open house party going almost all the time, and one night, as usual, a great crowd of writers, artists, and intellectuals had gathered for conversation, food, and drink. At 11:00, Lazarus ran the short distance to Gilder's house, not even bothering to put on a proper hat and veil. She pushed her way through the throng, ignoring the greetings of old friends. Finally, she found Richard Gilder, who was about to leave his own party and go to sleep.

She detained him. "Richard," she cried, "who is going to answer Madame Ragozin?"

He looked at the agitated young woman and answered simply, "You, of course."

As she became increasingly concerned with the plight of the Jewish refugees from Russia, Lazarus devoted all her energies to their cause. "I am all Israel's now," she said. "I have no thought . . . save for my own people."

SEVEN

Speaking Out

The plight of the Russian refugees, both in America and abroad, had transformed Lazarus's life. "I am all Israel's now," she proclaimed, "I have no thought, no passion, no desire save for my own people." Entering the public arena to fight for a cause was a difficult step for anyone to take—especially a 19th-century woman.

The fashions of the era reflected the prevalent notion that women should remain passive "homebodies." Tight, uncomfortable corsets made it nearly impossible for women to take a deep breath. Long, wide, hooped skirts restricted movement and picked up filth when worn out into the street. Thick woolen or cotton stockings, worn even during the summer, and bustles, which came in and out of fashion, added to the hot, cumbersome weight of proper feminine attire.

But the most serious obstacle a woman faced was the prevailing notion that females should be quiet and kind and should accept without question the opinions of their husbands, fathers, and brothers. Feminists such as Lucretia Mott and Elizabeth Cady Stanton were ridiculed as unnatural and overemotional when they publicly supported the notion that women should have the right to vote. Emily Dickinson, the American poet and Emma Lazarus's contemporary, spent her life as a virtual recluse. In one poem, she wistfully asks, "Why—do they shut me out of Heaven/Did I sing—too loud?"

Emma Lazarus complained of her frustration, too, in her poem "Echoes," which was written in 1880 but not published until after her death. "Veiled and screened by womanhood," as she

In the years preceding the Civil War, Lucretia Mott (left) and Elizabeth Cady Stanton became involved in feminism when male abolitionists discouraged them from participating in the antislavery movement.

put it, she was unable to write the kind of "manly" poetry appropriate to the modern age.

As she embarked on her campaign against anti-Semitism, Lazarus must have been aware of the unhappy fate that befell another female champion of the Jews, an unconventional actress named Adah Isaacs Menken. When a newspaper called *The Israelite* began to publish her stirring calls for a rekindling of Jewish pride and the granting

of full civil rights to Jews in the countries where these were denied them, Menken was briefly acclaimed as a heroine, and was much in demand as a speaker and lecturer.

Her public image soon changed, however. Menken was much too modern and liberated a woman by 19th-century standards. She wore her hair short and smoked cigarettes in public, but that was the least of it. Menken scandalized audiences in Europe and

This illustration gives a front and back view of a typical 19th-century outfit for middle-class women. The era's restrictive fashions reflected the prevalent notion that a woman's place was in the home.

America with stage performances in which she often appeared scantily clad. Her behavior was outrageous for the time, and her unfavorable reputation was sealed by false allegations that she was a prostitute.

But if Menken's fate alarmed Lazarus, the success of Mary Ann Evans, another unconventional woman, inspired her. The 19th century British novelist used the pen name George Eliot, because she feared that her writing would not be taken seriously if the public knew her books were written by a woman. But Mary Ann Evans made few other concessions to public opinion. When the man she loved could not divorce his wife, she lived with him without benefit of marriage. This arrangement, along with her liberal views, branded her an outcast.

Lazarus was certainly more conventional than Evans, but she admired her greatly. Lazarus kept a photograph of

Adah Isaacs Menken reclines on a fur rug for this publicity still. The flamboyant actress was controversial not only for her revealing costumes and liberated ways but also for her outspoken support of the Jewish cause.

the novelist on her desk for inspiration and even recommended that a refugee settlement in New Jersey be named "Eliot." Lazarus respected Evans because even though she was a Christian, she was an eloquent defender of the Jews. She died in 1880, before the Russian pogroms, but she had understood the threat of anti-Semitism even while many Jews, including the Lazarus family, had not been able to imagine that such atrocities could occur in the modern world. Her 1876 novel *Daniel Deronda* exposed anti-Semitic prejudice in English society and ad-

vanced a new, somewhat shocking idea: The Jewish people should build their own nation.

In 1882, Lazarus joined the ranks of these controversial spokeswomen for the Jewish cause with her rebuttal to Ragozin's accusations in *Century* magazine. Lazarus answered the Russian historian's charges in a beautifully written piece that tempered its outrage with dazzling rhetoric. "Murder, rape, arson, 100,000 families reduced to homeless beggary and the destruction of $80 million worth of property—such, in fewer words, are the acts for which an excuse is sought," she wrote. She attacked Ragozin's article for blaming the victims while excusing the perpetrators. She also posed a rhetorical question: "The dualism of the Jews is the dualism of humanity; they are made up of the good and the bad. May not Christendom be divided into those Christians who denounce such outrages as we are considering, and those who commit or apologize for them?"

Lazarus continued to draw public attention later that year, when she began publishing a series of essays in the *American Hebrew*. The pieces, collectively entitled *An Epistle to the Hebrews*, were thought-provoking and controversial. In them she attacked anti-Semitism and encouraged American Jews to band together. Speaking from experience, she also criticized the tendency of American Jews to deny their religious and ethnic pride in order to fit in with U.S. society. Years before efforts were made to establish a Jewish nation in Palestine, Lazarus spoke out for its establishment. This last position provoked great debate. Some Jewish leaders believed that if Jews started talking about nationhood, they would arouse suspicions all over the world, as the countries where they lived would begin to doubt their loyalty. But Lazarus went on publicizing the idea and gaining wider acceptance for it. She helped create the climate in which, 15 years later, Theodor Herzl

Although born a Christian, Mary Ann Evans championed the Jewish people in her novel Daniel Deronda. *Lazarus kept a photograph of Evans, who used the pen name George Eliot, on her desk for inspiration.*

could organize the First Zionist Congress and launch the movement that would eventually lead to the establishment of the nation of Israel.

Emma Lazarus's pride and involvement in Judaism also infused her poetry with a new vigor. In 1882 she

Hungarian-born journalist Theodor Herzl followed Lazarus's footsteps when he promoted the idea of a Jewish homeland. International anti-Semitism in the 1880s led to the Zionist movement, which worked to establish a Jewish state in Palestine.

published a new volume of poetry entitled *Songs of a Semite*. One of the verses in this collection, "The Crowing of the Red Cock," is an impassioned attack on violence committed in the name of religion. The poem begins:

Across the Eastern sky has glowed
  The flicker of a blood-red dawn,
Once more the clarion cock has crowed,
Once more the sword of Christ is
  drawn,
A million burning rooftrees light
The world-wide path of Israel's flight.

In other poems from *Songs of a Semite*, she called on Jews who, like

her family, had fallen away from their people, exhorting them to return to Judaism in this time of crisis. "The Banner of the Jew" includes the lines: "Oh for Jerusalem's trumpet now,/To blow a blast of shattering power,/To wake the sleepers high and low,/And rouse them to the urgent hour!"

Lazarus backed up her spirited words with action. In October 1883, when hundreds of Jewish refugees rioted on Ward's Island in a protest over conditions there, Lazarus argued on their behalf, complaining about insufficient food, a lack of running water and washing facilities, and the rubble-strewn and muddy ground which was the only place the children had to play. She overcame her shyness to speak on behalf of the refugees at numerous committee meetings, although at large gatherings she still handed over her speeches for someone else to read. She was a woman with a cause, and as such, she forgot the inhibitions she had grown up with—at least many of them.

Modern women may criticize Emma Lazarus for being timid, for not taking more risks, but the fact remains that her balancing act worked. Because she managed to remain a "respectable" woman despite some of her controversial opinions, her ideas and poems received wide circulation. She was able to gain new friends and supporters in intellectual and artistic circles that she

English writer Robert Browning had a great interest in Hebrew literature and culture. Lazarus met Browning during her 1883 trip abroad, and the two poets soon became good friends.

Herzl organized the First Zionist Congress, which was held in Basel, Switzerland, in 1897 "to secure for the Jewish people a home in Palestine guaranteed by public law." The Zionist dream was realized in 1948, with the creation of Israel.

never could have entered had she been branded a radical.

As Lazarus gained confidence, she continued to expand her horizons. In May 1883, at age 33, she at last fulfilled a childhood dream. Accompanied by her sister Annie, she boarded a ship for England.

German-born rabbi Gustav Gottheil gave her letters of introduction to many important people on the other side of the Atlantic, but she hardly needed his assistance. Her recent book of poetry, *Songs of a Semite*, had appeared in England and many people were eager to meet her. Robert Browning, the poet, was among them. Like Mary Ann Evans, Browning was an English intellectual with pro-Jewish sympathies. His father had worked for the Rothschilds, a Jewish banking family, and had liked and respected his employers. He passed that good feeling on to his son. One of Browning's best

Socialist writer and artist William Morris was another acquaintance Lazarus made during her trip to Europe. After visiting his innovative factory at Merton Abbey, Lazarus was inspired to help found New York's Hebrew Technical Institute.

known poems, "Rabbi Ben Ezra," presented an admiring view of an aging Jewish sage.

Browning had studied Hebrew, as had Lazarus, and they enjoyed reading and discussing difficult passages from traditional Hebrew sources together. He was also interested to hear of her experiences with the Russian refugees, and she was deeply moved to see Browning's continued devotion to the memory of his wife, the poet Elizabeth Barrett Browning, who had died 20 years previously.

Another high point of Lazarus's trip was meeting poet and social reformer William Morris. Both Lazarus and Morris felt torn between a love of art and an equally compelling commitment to social justice. Both had tried to find a way to combine the two. Morris did it by establishing handicrafts workshops at Merton Abbey, where he trained workers to make such items as rugs, chairs, and chandeliers. In keeping with his socialist philosophy, all the workers at Merton Abbey had a share in the profits.

Lazarus visited Morris's workshops twice and showed great interest. She was convinced that the Russian-Jewish refugees who had no inclination for farm work could better support themselves if they were trained in the manual arts. On her return from Europe, Lazarus would be the driving force behind the creation of New York City's

Hebrew Technical Institute. As a contemporary publication reported, the teenage boys who studied there learned not only the use of tools, but were also instructed on a wide variety of subjects "to make the boys think for themselves."

Lazarus also shared Morris's conviction that art should be for everyone, not just for the privileged few. The little girl who did not know what "poor" meant had grown into a woman who specifically asked her publisher to bring out her book, *Songs of a Semite*, in a cheap, no-frills edition so that it would not be beyond the means of ordinary people.

Not only was Lazarus stimulated by the new acquaintances she met in Great Britain, but the English countryside itself met all her expectations. Finally, she was able to see the towering cathedrals, majestic rivers, and multicolored fields she had read about in novels and poetry since childhood. "I drink in," she wrote, "at every sense, the sights, sounds, and smells, and the unimaginable beauty of it all." Despite the pleasures of travel, Lazarus could not bring herself to stay away from her family, especially her father, for long. She was back in New York by fall.

It was on her return that William Evarts asked her to help with the fundraising drive for the Statue of Liberty pedestal. At the time, Liberty's arm was on display in New York City's Madison

The torch-bearing arm of Bartholdi's Liberty Enlightening the World *is displayed in New York City's Madison Square Park in 1883, the same year Lazarus wrote her ode to the statue.*

Square Park not far from the Lazarus home, but the rest of the statue was still surrounded by scaffolding in a Paris warehouse. Although Lazarus found it difficult to write about a work of art that she had never seen, she drew on her recent experiences with the refugees to write a heartfelt poem that would eventually have a lasting impact.

Around the same time she composed "The New Colossus," she wrote another poem that drew on the same rich imagery that inspired her most famous verse. The second poem, entitled "1492," spoke of the momentous year in which Jews were expelled from Spain and the New World was discovered. In "1492" she wrote:

> Close-locked was every port, barred every gate.
> Then smiling, thou unveil'dst, O two-faced year,
> A virgin world where doors of sunset part,
> Saying, "Ho, all who are weary, enter here!"

Ironically, Emma Lazarus never realized the importance of "The New Colossus," or knew that in later years her fame would rest on this single poem. She was just glad that the poem was done in time for the fund-raiser and that William Evarts was pleased with it.

On December 3, 1883, the cream of New York society gathered at the National Academy of Design and paid admission to see the grand opening of the Pedestal Fund Art Loan Exhibition. On display were some of the finest works of art in private collections in the city. Singers arranged themselves on the grand staircase and sang French composer Charles-François Gounod's "Hymn to Liberty." That night, a portfolio of original writings contributed especially for the occasion was auctioned for $1,500. Before the bidding started, the verses in the collection, among them "The New Colossus," were read aloud.

It seems that Emma Lazarus was not among the guests. Perhaps she was uncomfortable, as ever, with the limelight, or it may be that she was already beginning to feel the effects of the illness, never definitely diagnosed, that began to sap her strength by summertime. She did not seem to be seriously sick but always suffered from fatigue.

Soon after her poem was read aloud at the Pedestal Fund Art Loan Exhibition, Lazarus received a letter from the poet and statesman James Russell Lowell. "I like your sonnet about the Statue, much better than I like the Statue itself," he wrote. "But your sonnet gives its subject a *raison d'être* [reason to be] which it wanted before quite as much as it wants a pedestal. You have set it on a noble one, saying

Bartholdi (second from right) oversees work on a plaster cast of the Statue of Liberty. After it was completed and erected in America, his masterpiece became a national emblem.

admirably just the right word to be said, an achievement more arduous than that of the sculptor." Lazarus was flattered by Lowell's words, but thought little about them. She had no idea that he had foreseen what no one else—least of all herself—had. "The New Colossus" would one day be as famous as Lady Liberty herself.

Just as Lazarus's lingering illness began to lift, another, more serious blow fell. On March 9, 1885, Moses Lazarus, the person Emma Lazarus cared for most in the world, died. From her letters, journals, and poetry,

it seems that no one else even came close in her esteem. Although he had done his best to keep his daughter physically and emotionally cloistered, Moses Lazarus had given his daughter the intellectual freedom and a love of ideas that served her well all her life.

After Mr. Lazarus's death, the family encircled the deathbed while his favorite daughter, though all but undone by grief, recited some sorrowful lines from Poe: "Ah, broken is the golden bowl! the spirit flown forever!/Let the bell toll!—a saintly soul floats on the Stygian river!"

The massive Statue of Liberty dwarfs passing schooners in New York Harbor. This print was made in 1885, when the 151-foot copper monument was still being shipped to America piece by piece.

EIGHT

"I Lift My Lamp Beside the Golden Door"

Alight but steady drizzle was falling over New York City on October 28, 1886, as 20,000 marchers paraded down Fifth Avenue to welcome Frédéric-Auguste Bartholdi and his majestic statue to America. U.S. president Grover Cleveland joined the sculptor on the reviewing stand, where they watched the parade. Then they traveled to Bedloe's Island for the long-awaited unveiling of *Liberty Enlightening the World*.

The statue was covered by a huge French flag as the ceremonies began. Dignitaries such as William Evarts made speeches about freedom and about the special relationship between France and the United States. At last came the moment Bartholdi had waited and worked for most of his life. From his place on a special platform,

the sculptor pulled a cord which drew aside the French tricolor. Unveiled, Lady Liberty looked out for the first time on America, her home.

Emma Lazarus did not witness this historic moment. In fact, the only women who were permitted to attend the Bedloe's Island ceremony were relatives of the French guests. But Lazarus could not have attended anyway. On October 28, she was far from New York.

Following her father's death, Lazarus had become deeply depressed. Everything made her think of her father, every room of the house, every familiar New York scene. Now that he was gone, Lazarus realized that she had depended on him not only in her personal life but in her professional life as well. As her sister Josephine re-

marked, "Her father's sympathy and pride in her work had been her *chief incentive* and ambition, and had spurred her on when her own confidence and spirit failed." As a poet and spokeswoman for the Jews, she was still in great demand. But she had trouble concentrating on her work; in fact she had difficulty getting through each day. After eight weeks of deep depression, Lazarus had decided to return to Europe, hoping that travel and new sights would distract her from her grief.

In Europe, her moods swung back and forth between great extremes of sorrow and joy. While in England, her first stop, she began work on her novel but gave up the project after finishing just one chapter. Overcome with despair, she wrote, "I have neither ability, energy, nor purpose. It is impossible to do anything...." Convinced that new scenery would revive her flagging spirits, she traveled to Holland that fall, and saw the works of the Dutch painter Rembrandt for the first time. Inspired by his works, she took up painting and found that her new vocation lifted her mood. Next she traveled on to Paris, then Rome, where she

New York Harbor is illuminated by fireworks during the unveiling of Liberty Enlightening the World, *which took place on October 28, 1886.*

This portrait by the 17th-century Dutch painter Rembrandt shows his characteristic mastery of light and shadow. During her second trip to Europe, Lazarus was so moved by Rembrandt's work that she took up painting herself.

declared that "a whole new world of sensation" had been opened to her. The ancient statues she saw everywhere in that city were so marvelous to her that she lost her newfound interest in painting and resolved to study sculpture instead. Between these emotional high points, she plunged back into inertia and despair.

Lazarus next returned to England for another visit to Robert Browning. She held the poet in high esteem, and perhaps she enjoyed hearing about his late wife, with whom she had so much in common. When Browning first met Elizabeth Barrett, she was a 39-year-old invalid who was kept a virtual prisoner by her tyrannical father. They married and fled together to Italy where the mild climate and a more normal life improved her delicate health. The couple became famous all over the world, not only for their poetry, but for the dramatic story of their courtship.

Elizabeth Barrett Browning and Lazarus were both poets; like Browning, Lazarus had also been overly sheltered and sickly as a child. Both had been strongly tied to their fathers, though in Lazarus's case, the bond was not tyranny but love. And in 1886, Lazarus was 37 years old, two years younger than Elizabeth Barrett had been when Robert Browning offered her a new life away from her father.

A new life without her father—that

There were many parallels between the life of Elizabeth Barrett Browning (above) and Emma Lazarus. Both led sheltered childhoods, had powerful fathers, and expressed their feelings through poetry.

was exactly what Emma Lazarus needed to find. She tried to find it in art, and she may indeed have harbored the hope that she might one day find a Robert Browning of her own.

One day that summer, as she was wandering in England's Malvern Hills, she suddenly came upon the place where Elizabeth Barrett Browning had

Nineteenth-century Parisians stroll in front of the Louvre art museum. Despite her declining health, Lazarus visited the museum often during her stay in France.

once seen a tree struck by lightning. As she stood upon the very spot, Emma Lazarus felt a terrible jolt of pain shoot through her body.

The sensation she experienced was not the result of a mystical communion with Browning; it was a symptom of the disease that would soon cut her life short. In the days that followed, she was bothered by pains all over her body and had trouble swallowing and digesting her food.

Thinking that these new problems might be no more than signs of her continuing depression, she dragged herself from her sickbed and returned to Holland. Soon she felt so much better that she began writing a book about Rembrandt. She journeyed to France next, where one day she happened to see an English-language newspaper that described the unveiling of the Statue of Liberty, but all of that seemed to be part of another world.

By this time, she was chronically exhausted, and the pains had returned, much worse than before. Emma Lazarus learned that she was suffering from something more deadly than depression. She had Hodgkin's disease, a form of cancer. Her sister Josephine traveled to France to watch over her sister and encourage her to seek treatments. Lazarus was determined to ignore her declining health and spent her time in the vast galleries of Paris's Louvre museum. She had decided that she would spend her last days on earth not with doctors, but among beautiful artworks.

At her sister's urging, Lazarus finally agreed to return home. They sailed for New York on July 23, the day after her 38th birthday. On the last day of that month, their ship reached New York Harbor after nightfall. Because of the darkness, Emma Lazarus never laid eyes on the Statue of Liberty, the towering symbol she called "The New Colossus."

Despite her illness, Lazarus continued to write. While she was still in Europe, she had written a series of poems about the "Jewish reality and the Jewish dream," published in March of 1887. Even though she was bedridden after her return to New York, she continued to work on translations of Italian poetry. Lazarus's sister Josephine noted that "Her intellect seemed kindled anew, and none but those who saw her during the last supreme ordeal can realize that wonderful flash of fire of the spirit before its extinction.... She talked about art, poetry, the scenes of travel, of which her brain was so full."

Emma Lazarus's life had come full circle. As it had done during her childhood and adolescence, her mind roamed free while she remained confined at home. Emma Lazarus died on November 19, 1887. America and Europe mourned her passing. John Greenleaf Whittier, a poet, remarked that "her people will mourn the death of this woman, but they will not be alone. At her grave the tears of the daughters of Jerusalem will mingle with those of the Christians." From England, Robert Browning professed his "admiration for the genius and love of the character of my lamented friend." The poet Walt Whitman expressed regret that he had never met Lazarus, writing that, "She must have had a great, sweet, unusual nature."

Gradually, however, Lazarus's reputation began to wane, and her poems were read less frequently. Some members of her family thought this was just as well. They had been embarrassed over her deep involvement in Jewish causes and her association with what they considered to be crude, uneducated refugees. Her youngest sister, Annie, a convert to Catholicism, held the copyright to much of Emma Lazarus's work and also owned many of her sister's personal papers. She considered much of Lazarus's work "sectarian propaganda" rather than literature, and she was unwilling to see it

The enigmatic face of the Statue of Liberty is actually a likeness of Frédéric-Auguste Bartholdi's mother. Lazarus's stirring poem about the monument gave it a new identity as the "Mother of Exiles."

Emma Lazarus succumbed to Hodgkin's disease on November 19, 1887. After her death, poet John Greenleaf Whittier wrote that "the Semitic race has had no braver singer."

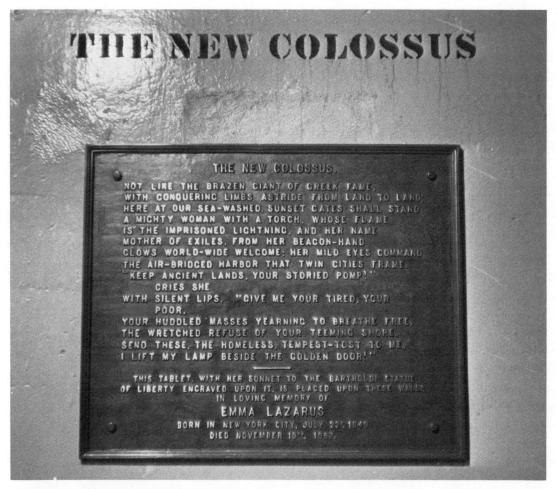

This bronze tablet inscribed with "The New Colossus" was installed on the base of the Statue of Liberty in 1903. Today, more than 1 million visitors to the monument see the poem each year.

reprinted. She never published her sister's personal papers or made them available to scholars, and they have since disappeared.

Despite this obstacle, the power of Lazarus's vision ensured that she would not slip into obscurity. On May 5, 1903, more than 15 years after the poet's death, a woman named Georgiana Schuyler had the words of "The New Colossus" engraved on a bronze tablet and installed just inside the entrance to the pedestal of the Statue of Liberty, where it can still be seen. For immigrants and American citizens alike, her poem gives the statue its meaning. As journalist Estelle F. Kleiger noted recently, "It was the genius of French sculptor Frédéric Auguste Bartholdi that gave form to *Liberty Enlightening the World*, but it took the pen of Emma Lazarus to give the goddess a voice—one that would speak a message of welcome and hope to millions seeking new lives in a land of opportunity."

Modern immigrants, most of whom arrive by airplane, are still greeted with Lazarus's words of welcome, which have been inscribed on a marble plaque near the customs area of John F. Kennedy International Airport. Open door immigration policy continues to be controversial, but thanks in part to Emma Lazarus, the ideal of America as a haven is alive in the national consciousness today.

Lazarus's dedication to the Jewish people has also had a lasting impact. Her espousal of such causes as the creation of a Jewish homeland has born fruit in the 20th century. She did not live long enough to learn about Herzl's Zionist movement, or to see Israel, a Jewish nation, become a reality. Neither would she know that in spite of opposition, the U.S. government would allow close to 2 million Jewish immigrants into America by 1914.

Despite her privileged upbringing and her era's narrow ideas concerning women's role in society, Lazarus dedicated herself to helping people who were, in some respects, utterly unlike her. This was the goal of her life. "Until we are all free," Lazarus wrote, "we are none of us free."

THE WRITINGS OF EMMA LAZARUS

POETRY COLLECTIONS

Poems and Translations, 1867.

Admetus and Other Poems, 1871.

Songs of a Semite, 1882.

By the Waters of Babylon, 1887.

NOVEL

Alide, 1874.

VERSE TRAGEDY

The Spagnoletto, 1876.

FURTHER READING

Birmingham, Stephen. *The Grandees: America's Sephardic Elite*. New York: Harper & Row, 1971.

Howe, Irving. *World of Our Fathers: The Journey of the East European Jews to America and the Life They Found and Made*. New York: Harcourt Brace Jovanovich, 1976.

Jacob, Heinrich Edward. *The World of Emma Lazarus*. New York: Macmillan, 1964.

Lazarus, Emma. *Admetus*. Reprint of 1871 edition. New York: Gregg, 1971.

———. *The Letters of Emma Lazarus, 1868–1885*. Edited by Morris U. Scappes. New York: New York Public Library, 1949.

———. *Songs of a Semite*. Reprint of 1871 edition. New York: Gregg, 1971.

Levinson, Nancy Smiler. *I Lift My Lamp: Emma Lazarus and the Statue of Liberty*. New York: E. P. Dutton, 1986.

Merriam, Eve. *Emma Lazarus: Woman with a Torch*. New York: Citadel Press, 1956.

Shapiro, Mary J. *Gateway to Liberty: The Story of the Statue of Liberty and Ellis Island*. New York: Vintage Books, 1986.

Vogel, Dan. *Emma Lazarus*. Boston: Twayne Publishers, 1980.

CHRONOLOGY

July 22, 1849	Born Emma Lazarus in New York City
1867	Publishes first book, *Poems and Translations*
1868	Begins correspondence with Ralph Waldo Emerson
1871	Publishes *Admetus and Other Poems*, dedicated to Emerson
April 21, 1874	Death of her mother, Esther
1874	Lazarus suffers nervous breakdown
	Recovers and publishes *Alide*, her first novel
1876	Visits Emerson and family at Concord, Massachusetts
1876–81	Writes poems, translations, and critical articles for various journals
1882	Visits Russian-Jewish refugees on Ward's Island
	Responds to anti-Semitic attack published in *Century* magazine
	Publishes poetry anthology *Songs of a Semite*
1882–83	Writes a series of essays collectively entitled *An Epistle to the Hebrews*, for the *American Hebrew*
1883	Visits Europe; writes "The New Colossus"
March 9, 1885	Father, Moses, dies
1885–87	Lazarus travels in Europe
Nov. 19, 1887	Dies in New York
May 5, 1903	Plaque bearing the words of "The New Colossus" is affixed on pedestal of Statue of Liberty

INDEX

INDEX

PICTURE CREDITS

Diane Lefer has published two historical novels as well as many short stories and magazine articles. Her work has won recognition from the National Endowment for the Arts and the Library of Congress.

Matina S. Horner is president of Radcliffe College and associate professor of psychology and social relations at Harvard University. She is best known for her studies of women's motivation, achievement, and personality development. Dr. Horner serves on several national boards and advisory councils, including those of the National Science Foundation, Time Inc., and the Women's Research and Education Institute. She earned her B. A. from Bryn Mawr College and Ph.D. from the University of Michigan, and holds honorary degrees from many colleges and universities, including Mount Holyoke, Smith, Tufts, and the University of Pennsylvania.

261717

jB
LAZARUS

Lefer, Diane

Emma Lazarus

$16.95

DATE		

DEC 14 1988